salmonpoetry40

Publishing Irish & International Poetry Since 1981

She knew there were
days of clear light,
when time stretches the air.
She walked through them,
knew that they moved
through her...

from *Daughter* by Jessie Lendennie, first published by Salmon in 1988

for Fred with love & gratitude! Jessie

Days of Clear Light

A Festschrift in Honour of
Jessie Lendennie & in Celebration
of Salmon Poetry at 40

Edited by

ALAN HAYES & NESSA O'MAHONY

Published in 2021 by
Salmon Poetry
Cliffs of Moher, County Clare, Ireland
Website: www.salmonpoetry.com
Email: info@salmonpoetry.com

ISBN 978-1-912561-98-8

Cover Image: *Jessie Lendennie*
Cover Design & Typesetting: *Siobhán Hutson*

Printed in Ireland by Sprint Print

*Salmon Poetry gratefully acknowledges the support of
The Arts Council / An Chomhairle Ealaíon*

In Memory of

Little Zach, Zookie, Big Zach, Zena,
Cynthia Freckle, Shanny,
Sir Jack Silkcoat & Zeke

And for
Eve Catherine Hutson Jeanotte

CONTENTS

Michael D. Higgins

All those who appreciate the written or spoken word are greatly indebted to Jessie Lendennie, whose decision in 1981 to make Ireland her new home was a seminal moment in the literary and publishing life of Ireland. Her eclectic reach, her generous nurturing of new talent, and her great desire to see the names of writers in print, including new entrants in particular, has made an invaluable contribution in terms of access to Irish literature, and the discovery, emergence and appreciation of new and exciting literary voices.

Many highly regarded poets can trace their writing journey back to the *The Salmon Journal* and the Salmon Poetry Press, established from the vision, and sustained and developed from the hard work and, at times, heroism of Jessie Lendennie, whose assistance and encouragement from their launch has enabled so many literary careers to grow and flourish.

The Salmon Poetry Press has never shied from experimentalism. For Jessie, the world of publishing has always been a space of offering new possibilities and exciting opportunities. In exercising choice on what to publish, she has been unafraid to take a risk, to follow her heart and her instinct down roads untraveled. In doing so, she has also brought many readers down new pathways, introducing them to remarkable writers who may have remained undiscovered or 'off the beaten track' if it were not for Jessie.

It was in *The Salmon* journal I published thirty years ago, and Salmon Poetry Press published my first collection, *The Betrayal*.

This *Festschrift* is a deserved tribute to Jessie Lendennie and those at Salmon who support her. It is a great roll-call of some of Ireland and the world's best loved writers, along with newer talent that is there to be fully explored. It is a collection that speaks profoundly of Jessie's place in Ireland's literary community where she is viewed with great appreciation, and particularly by those to whom she gifted that most important of experiences—their first opportunity for publication. Jessie is spoken of with admiration and affection by so many other renowned writers who are fortunate to call Jessie a friend.

This gathering together of writers from Ireland and beyond to pay Jessie such an honour is so well deserved. May I join with all those whose work appears in this celebratory publication in paying tribute to Jessie Lendennie for all she has done to enrich the world of Irish writing and publishing.

May she have continued success as the Salmon Poetry Press marks this milestone anniversary.

Traoslaim leithí agus guidhim gach rath uirthi agus ar Salmon do'n todchaí.

Michael D. Higgins
PRESIDENT OF IRELAND

THE
SALMON

1981

AN INTERNATIONAL
LITERARY JOURNAL
FROM THE
WEST OF IRELAND

1982

1983

1984

Nessa O'Mahony

We writers can be a forgetful bunch. So caught up are we in our inner worlds, our visionary imaginations, we can sometimes take for granted the people and processes that bring our visions to the outside world. Significant anniversaries of publishers are thus an important opportunity to not only take stock but to express gratitude to the people who too often remain invisible and unacknowledged.

So when Alan Hayes and I were chatting in summer 2020 about Salmon Poetry's forthcoming 40th anniversary (in 2021), and the largely unacknowledged role that Salmon's publisher, Jessie Lendennie, has played in supporting and developing the careers of so many writers in Ireland and around the world, we knew we had to make something happen that would express appropriate appreciation for all that wonderful work. At that point we approached Siobhán Hutson, Salmon's production manager, who as it turns out had been discussing a similar plan for a festschrift with Salmon poet Patrick Chapman, so we put our collective heads together to make the idea a reality.

Because Salmon itself had marked its 35th anniversary in 2016 with a fantastic and inclusive anthology of poets published since its foundation in 1981 (*Even The Daybreak*), we didn't feel the need for another similar publication five years on. But we did want to create something more personal, a collection of voices that would make their own tribute to Jessie and her work: a festschrift of poetry, prose and memoir from both a sampling of 75 Salmon poets but also from the wider community of writers and commentators who wanted to share their own appreciation of Jessie's extraordinary achievements. There was a warm and enthusiastic response from those we approached, even from those few for whom the perilously tight deadline was too restrictive for them to be able to write something new and unpublished. Everyone we mentioned the project to was delighted that it was happening, that there would be a public expression of the widespread affection and admiration for Jessie and her work. All agreed to keep the project top secret; we knew the toughest part of this would be keeping it from Jessie. Indeed our fellow conspirator, Salmon Poetry's Siobhán Hutson, had to take many phone calls in her car in order to keep the project from her.

As the work poured in, the depth of that admiration and warmth for Jessie became apparent. In these pieces you'll find common themes—expressions of love and loss, of travel and adventure, of political commentary and cultural exploration. Salmon has always been a publisher of work from both sides of the Atlantic, and international voices continue to interweave with Irish ones here, as they have always done. And yes, there are many dogs, both spirit animals and the living ones so beloved of Jessie and many of her writers.

Sometimes the writer-publisher loses sight of their own writing. It was important, too, that there would be tributes to Jessie's own poetry, with poems that are in express dialogue with that work. Her lyricism, her compassion, determination and single-mindedness are echoed time and time again on these pages. We are so grateful to everyone who responded so generously to our call to contribute to this volume.

I want to give the last word here to one of those contributors by quoting from a poem that in fact we didn't end up choosing, but which contains a line that sums up so many of the qualities of Jessie Lendennie. In his poem 'Daughter', Richard W. Halperin writes 'I like poets for whom language is decency'. We have been so fortunate to enjoy Jessie Lendennie's 'decency' for the past 40 years—may there be many, many more.

EDITORIAL BY

Alan Hayes

Bringing the Injuns In: Jessie Lendennie, Salmon and the Irish Literary World

When one examines the Irish poetry world over the past forty years, it is evident that one individual has done more than any other to channel a more modern Ireland, to develop Irish literature, to move poetry forward, to launch new and diverse voices, and to bring large and appreciative audiences to poetry, locally, nationally and internationally. That person is Jessie Lendennie.

Lendennie is a visionary, an outsider, an American, a woman, a bohemian living on the west coast as far away as is possible from the centres of power in the arts world. Her experience of working in 1970s London in the Poetry Society gave her an insight into the damage that could be done by conservative voices and dysfunctional power structures. After moving to Ireland in 1981 she met a poetry world which needed a shake up. She had a vision to make it more relevant and more representative.

It has been said that Irish poetry has an 'inherited male tradition'. That statement—obviously—is incorrect. Women have always written and published, and a little research shows that Irish literature has often been more diverse than generally presumed. Early twentieth century Ireland had a large number of literary presses and, while male authors predominated, there was a significant amount of women also writing poetry, plays, fiction and criticism.

The latter half of the century brought a more traditional and conservative publishing climate. Dolmen Press was the pre-eminent literary publisher of poetry in Ireland from the 1950s until the late 1980s. In the 1960s and 1970s poets could also submit manuscripts to a number of small presses such as New Writers Press, Sáirséal agus Dill and Goldsmith, while mainstream presses such as Blackstaff and Gill occasionally published poetry. Generally, male poets were chosen (though Mercier did publish Nuala Ní Dhomhnaill's debut in 1981). The foundation by Peter Fallon of Tara Telephone and Gallery Press in 1970 was a major development with its distinctive classical, stylish and traditional volumes, though a gender imbalance was there from the beginning—in the 1970s alone over 30 male writers were published, and only one female (Eiléan Ní Chuilleanáin). In 1977 Dermot Bolger founded the influential Raven Arts Press, and over the next 15 years published important new, radical and working-class authors, although less than a handful were women. Arlen House published Eavan Boland's *In Her Own Image* (1980) and *Night Feed* (1982)—arguably the most groundbreaking collections from this time—though unfortunately the press's plans to address the dire situation facing women poets didn't come to fruition then. The energetic Irish language publisher Coiscéim, founded in 1980 by Pádraig Ó Snodaigh, published a very small number of women poets in the 1980s. Dedalus Press, founded in 1985 by John F Deane, published a large number of interesting new and traditional voices, though only a tiny number by women; this improved when the press was relaunched by Pat Boran in 2006. The most diverse list in the mid-1980s came from the tiny, poorly-funded Beaver Row Press (1982–1991) which published Eithne Strong, Leland Bardwell, Anne Hartigan, Lynda Moran, Glenda Cimino and Paula Meehan's debut and second collections. The evidence shows that the more funding available, the more traditional the publishing choices—the reasons why need to be further interrogated.

Thus when Jessie Lendennie decided in 1985 to start publishing poetry collections alongside *The Salmon* journal, she had to address an imbalanced Irish literary and publishing world which needed a major shake-up. The first Salmon collection was Eva Bourke's debut, *Gonella* (1985), launched by Michael D. Higgins in Galway. The following year saw *Goddess on the Mervue Bus* by Rita Ann Higgins, debut poetry by a working-class writer which sold in thousands, an unheard of feat in Irish poetry.

Over the following years Salmon published the debut collections by women who have become an integral part of the Irish and international literary world such as Mary O'Malley, Moya Cannon, Mary O'Donnell and Elaine Feeney; in fact over 100 debut authors have been launched to date. However, Salmon has never focused solely on women writers; indeed they have almost always had a relatively equal gender balance. They published the debut collection by Michael D. Higgins, President of Ireland; the debut

Two women, Two Shores

poems by medbh mcguckian and nuala archer

and second collections by Theo Dorgan, then director of Poetry Ireland; the debut and subsequent collections by Gerard Donovan, the Booker-nominated novelist; the debut collection by John O'Donohue (who later wrote the international bestseller *Anam Cara*); and the debut and subsequent collections by Eamonn Wall, one of the most prominent Irish Studies academics in the US. One of their earliest books, *Two Women, Two Shores* (1989), is an imaginative and experimental cross-Atlantic collaboration between American poet Nuala Archer and Belfast visionary Medbh McGuckian. Indeed, Salmon was the first mainstream Irish press to publish McGuckian, who has subsequently published with Gallery Press and Arlen House.

Salmon also does not only confine its work to poetry; Patricia Forde's debut young adult novel, *Tír faoi Thoinn/The Land Beneath the Sea*, first appeared in 1991; Patricia Burke Brogan's revolutionary play about a Magdalene laundry, *Eclipsed*, was first published in 1994 and reissued many times; *In the Chair*, John

Brown's fascinating collection of interviews with poets from the North of Ireland, including Heaney, Longley, Montague, Mahon and McGuckian, appeared in 2002; and Joan McBreen's anthology, *The White Page/An Bhileog Bhán: Twentieth Century Irish Women Poets* (1999) is a critical and crucial piece of scholarship which has gone into multiple editions.

Lendennie has always been interested in international voices, and Salmon has published world-renowned writers such as Adrienne Rich, Ray Bradbury, Carol Ann Duffy, Robin Skelton, Jean Valentine, Marvin Bell and Eavan Boland. Lendennie has also honoured an older generation of poets such as Eithne Strong, James Liddy, Leland Bardwell and Robert Greacen. Through *The Salmon* journal, numerous anthologies and individual collections, Lendennie has also published and supported a number of other publisher/poets including Dermot Bolger, Pat Boran, Seamus Cashman, Glenda Cimino, Patrick Cotter, John F. Deane, Peter Fallon, David Gardiner and Knute Skinner. In the early 1990s Salmon entered into an association with Poolbeg Press in Dublin which resulted in new editions of crucial titles. Salmon became independent again in 1996 and has enjoyed a happy twenty five years based near the Cliffs of Moher in County Clare and, since 2012, at The Salmon Bookshop & Literary Centre in Ennistymon, Co. Clare. Jessie works there with Siobhán Hutson, whose imaginative design work has raised Salmon's profile and reputation as one of the finest poetry publishers in the world.

The Salmon list is truly diverse on grounds of gender, age, race, religion and sexuality (with a wide list of LGBTQ+ writers). Lendennie has always supported poets from throughout the entire island of Ireland, and she has published writers from at least twenty countries worldwide. For Jessie, it has always been about the poems. She looks beyond egos, tempers, tantrums and betrayals and—by focusing on the poetry—she finds herself always able to work with people (I won't even try to claim I have that same level of patience!).

In an opinion piece written for *Poetry Ireland* in 2002, Lendennie gives a succinct analysis of an Irish literary world which was 'keeping the injuns out', while she was trying to integrate the 'injuns' with everyone else. There was criticism of Salmon's list being too diverse and indeed there was at least one attempt to refuse funding and close down the press due to this. Now, in 2021, diversity is the key buzzword in the arts world, with enormous amounts of funding being offered to 'do diversity'. Hopefully, we will come to a stage where there is a better understanding of the concepts and realities of equality, when a balance will be found and true and lasting integration will take place. At its core, quality of writing is the key. It is ironic that Salmon was the first to embrace diversity in a real and integral sense, and that profound desire to address equality caused damage to the press. However, Jessie Lendennie continues on, and she has done more than anybody else to open up the world of Irish poetry to move it away from its narrow, old, pale, male, stale provincialism. She has literally introduced the world to Irish poetry and us to the world.

The late, much-lamented poet Eavan Boland named Salmon as:

> one of the most innovative, perceptive and important publishing houses in the UK and Ireland. It has fostered and supported the work of new writers and has established them in the public consciousness.

And according to Fintan O'Toole, Salmon:

> has become unquestionably the most important publisher of poetry in Ireland. The publishing of poetry has always been a venture which requires courage, dedication and imagination, since it is very seldom a straightforward commercial enterprise. With very few exceptions, poetry books are unlikely ever to be bestsellers. Yet anyone with an interest in the arts knows that poetry has an influence on many more immediately popular forms. The voices that are given expression in poetry go on to re-echo through fiction, theatre and even popular music, and this has been even more obviously the case in recent years in Ireland. In

this sense, Salmon has been an essential seed-bed, not alone for Irish poetry, but also for a much wider spread of artistic activity. No one else in Ireland in the last few years has been as prepared as Salmon to publish previously unknown poets. Salmon has not merely accommodated new voices, it has actively sought them out. And the general cultural significance of this work has been made immeasurably more important by Salmon's innovation in discovering and publishing the work of so many women. Poetry has been arguably the most important mode of expression for a new generation of Irish women writers, and Salmon has been the most important channel of that expression. In this light, though it has itself been a small and quiet enterprise, Salmon's work in recent years has been of large and loud importance. Salmon has done Galway, Irish poetry and Irish women proud, demonstrating the great significance of forces that might have seemed to be outside the mainstream. It is important to Irish culture as a whole that that spirit should not only survive but grow and blossom.

We owe a huge debt of gratitude to Jessie Lendennie for all that she has gifted us through her stewardship of Salmon over these past forty years.

Days *of*
Clear Light

MICHAEL ALLEN

Skin like a baby's

for Eamonn

When I handed you the poem,
the one which claims that skin remembers,
you read it, folded it and placed it in your pocket,
as if suppressing evidence you feared might do me harm.
Then you talked about your mother and her final days.
"The young ones don't want to hear it," you said,
"but her skin had become like a baby's."

And you were telling me more, but I had gone away
back to the time I kissed my father goodnight, the first time in years,
and came up short, shocked by the softness of his stubble-less skin.
He felt the tactless question of my hesitation,
"The only good thing with these drugs," he said, "no need to shave anymore."
And I was back too with all the goodnight kisses of my whole childhood,
where his bristled, evening chin against my softness
measured the space between us.

And then you reached across the table and grabbed me by the ears,
held them tight and pulled
me back into the story you were telling,
about how you had been changing your mother's clothes and she,
so near to death, had grabbed you just like that, by the ears
and laughing at you like the boy you had been, rolled you over
    on your back,
in her soft-skinned arms, announcing in triumph,
"I have you now. I have you."

So here is new evidence against us both. This you cannot fold away.
Two men, sitting in a bar, exchanging poems
and struggling to find a way to live near the surface of our
    time-roughened skins,
close enough to feel the memories of all the kinds of love
and stay there, open to what may still be offered, until

time scoops us up by the ears, softening us
back to where we started, declaring:
I have you now. I have you.

MARCK L. BEGGS

Suspension

The birds are not socially isolating.
The weather wears off like old glue.
An invisible foe takes hold of our pulse
to measure the beat of fear,
to smell the hardening of our will.

On Woodlawn Avenue, the house
next to Temple Hall crumbles
at the speed of mulch feeding the aged dirt.
It is a place to stand among wraiths
and observe shadows cast from ash.

We discuss the air as if snow
were in the forecast, as if a breeze
could push apart our hands. It is the sorrow
of the ages inviting the bell to sing.
It is the hum escaping our lips.

DERMOT BOLGER

The Poet as Golfer

for Jessie

So many evenings loitering on fairways
Trying to instil in my sons these tricks:
Do not grip too tightly in your stance
Or flex your shoulders lest they stiffen up,
But swing with a relaxed smooth tempo
And allow the actual club to do the work.

Really I should have been teaching myself,
Because I'm only slowly learning as a poet
To realign my posture, ease my mind of tension,
Place myself at the mercy of the unexpected,
Trust my imagination to find its own tempo
And allow the words that come to do the work.

EVA BOURKE

Dear Jessie, when I think of us,
how young we were! If only ...

... we could have just another one or even five minutes of those days,
(but let's not be greedy), when our hair was blond or red or black and
    our dresses
were loose and light, six of us or more, a circle of friends in the lamp's glow
inside a lit-up circle of words, the streets in our small town
wet and dark, the day tasting of rain water and salt.
I'd love just one more of those days that weighed light,
with us arguing about nothing less substantial, nothing
of more consequence than a line in a poem—an obscure or jarring line,
or a word picked up on a street corner, or left behind
in a rumpled bed, an appeal stuck to a mirror, a word
birthed by a clammy sea like a bag of sludge, a word
that took to the air like the colourful kites the kids let fly
on the swamp near your house. We sailed
in that rickety boat of language and you'd be the one setting the sails
with the calm assurance of a mariner.
Jessie, forgive me, in a watery city like Galway
where the sea rises a little each year,
the nautical metaphors are as plentiful as flotsam found on the strand.
I remember your loose-fitting dresses you'd cut out from patterns,
fusible, interfacing, wide trim and flap and single fold,
poplin strewn with flowers, lawn, linen, spotted silk;
there was as much finesse and craft in your dresses
as in the complex patterning of a verse,
and I used to imagine a poem that came easy,
a poem I could live in like a favourite dress, something light and loose.
When I think of you now, so many decades later,
mother of poets, up in your clifftop aerie,
where the cliff face below you is patterned white
with the gentle streaks of bird shit left by world-travelling birds,

I see you walking with your trusted sheepdogs,
more a flock than a pack in this wind-swept precipitous place,
with puffins and kittiwakes, razorbills and guillemots for company
as well as the odd fiach dubh, the stern priestly raven,
cruising the thermals or winging it back to his nest of sticks.
Dear Jessie, we owe you a life time's gratitude,
you built your house of poetry with love and persistence over the years,
made from patterns of words, of lines that connect worlds,
a house with room for so many to live in:
welcoming, spacious, airy, light.

HEATHER BRETT

How clever the Indoctrination of the Innocents

for Cory

So
the oceans have receded to find
their own level,
and carcasses of shopping trolleys lie exhausted
on moraines of guilt
seagull skeletons are all barbs and beak
rotted planks return to pulp
flotsam waits quietly in small, separated
swells.

I'm surprised life still surprises me.
Still silences me.
Still knifes me in the heart.
Still drops the whole sky on me,
soft but lethal. I can't breathe.
Nurture overcomes nature
at every milestone and
the blessed are wrestled to the dirt,
the dust swallowing a phantom.
Upright, the shallow brush themselves off
and walk away.
They walk to the dark matter of
pretence, reach for the hand
of bias, their first words, though
they don't know it, are bigotry.
All their lives they are given; given
just enough care to react;
just enough information to steer them
well away from the truth,

shown just enough miracles that they have
the faith without question.
The begging bowl of their soul is full
and heavy with small slights and
sour tokens of war
and they see themselves magnified
and multiplied *ad infinitum*
in the mirrors of righteousness.

Of course I blame myself!
Love is no excuse to pardon repeated
retreats behind the rank and file
of the superficial, the phoney,
the false.
We all play to the gallery,
the motives caught in the dancing spotlights
are like stars, or diamonds, sweet wrappers, or fairy dust:
you can never tell what is real
what is not

BARBARA BROWN

Jessie

'You must meet Jessie!'

I knew who Jessie was: Jessie Lendennie, Publisher and Managing Director of Salmon Poetry, located at the Cliffs of Moher, Co. Clare, the foremost female publisher in Ireland and, like me, an American.

In 2001 Maurice Harmon and I were in his study looking at poems for his first Salmon poetry collection. He had published three chapbooks, *The Book of Precedence* and *A Stillness at Kiawah*, 1996, both with Three Spires Press, and *Tales of Death*, Lapwing, 2000; but this was his first book-length poetry collection. And. although I sensed that Maurice was unlikely to show strong emotion, I knew he was pleased that Jessie Lendennie had accepted *The Last Regatta* for publication: 'You must come with me and Maura tonight to Jessie's launch.'

I do not remember the books launched that night at the Irish Writers Centre in Dublin nor the poets who read, but I remember Jessie's presence and her introduction. Slightly husky voice, no notes, off-the-cuff delivery, bright blue eyes sparkling, enthusiastic description of her poets and their books. Meeting Jessie that night was the start of a nineteen-year personal association and friendship. During those years I have valued her skill as editor, for example, as we prepared Maurice's next five collections for publication, the seventh, *afterwords*, in 2020. And after Jessie opened the successful Salmon Bookshop and Literary Centre at Ennistymon, I was fortunate to be able to spend pleasant weeks living and working there.

During those years I also observed the significant growth of Salmon Poetry and of The Salmon Bookshop & Literary Centre, evidenced by the broad range of books in the window giving artistic support to established writers but also to new names.

Salmon: A Journey in Poetry—25 Years of Publishing, 2007, a landmark publication, heralded books by, among others, Eva Bourke and Rita Ann Higgins—books, published by Salmon in the mid-1980s which broke new ground for women poets. Since then over 600 books of poetry have been published by well-known Irish poets such as Moya Cannon, Theo Dorgan, Mary O'Malley and Mary O'Donnell, Fred Johnston and Eamonn Wall and by international poets, Carol Ann Duffy, Adrienne Rich, Ron Houchin and Marvin Bell, among others, as well as many debut collections from young poets. Today, I am pleased to be part of this festschrift honouring Jessie and Salmon's forty years of publishing in Ireland.

SIOBHÁN CAMPBELL

Independence

for Jessie Lendennie

Edged with cliffs, and reasons not to slip,
landslides in waiting, a temper of muds.
The rights of passage, the right to build
a stile between these fields, was gained.
Below the cliff, a basking shark on days
before the tourists come, is motionless
thinking its own thoughts.
Once a puffin, etched in silhouette,
a profile stark against the rock,
its colours fading as the sun declined.

Where sound of sea, sound of tides changing
where river of wind, breath of seasons turning
where trees become themselves each spring
the spirits gather and the poem survives
kept holy by the keeper—

who once brought a live lobster
home in a box to cook, then let it go,
who tried to save the crooked trees
from bending to their deaths,
who sowed the seeds of wild-flowers
so the solitary bee could nest
in thistle, bramble, high hollowed stem—
wherever the long-won song is hummed,
laying wrapped larvae in a nectar bed.
Each year the offspring rise to pollinate again.

1985

GONELLA

Poems by Eva Bourke
Drawings by Jay Murphy

RITA ANN HIGGINS

GODDESS ON THE
MERVUE BUS

1986

1987

1988

MOYA CANNON

The Orange Rucksack

'They change their sky, not their soul,
who rush across the sea'
—Horace

It will soon be fifty years since I waited
at the carousel in Orly airport
for an orange rucksack, bought
in an army surplus shop in Liffey Street.

With its new-nylon stiffness and smell,
it whispered Versailles, art, romance,
the wing-wide world and a transfigured me.
I stuffed it full of anxieties and mended jeans.

When, at last, it nudged past
the hawk-watched plastic flaps
one of its orange ties had opened
and it had begun to spill out its innards.

It looked brasher, cheaper than the other baggage.
I caught it as it tried to trundle past, trussed it up,
hefted it onto my back and stepped out,
terrified and happy, into the hot Parisian afternoon.

HÉLÈNE CARDONA

Wind Spirit

I glide down all steps of the amphitheater
my own mother and father
spirit to source

The force of me comes from under the ocean
tsunami, all encompassing

I travel from darkness to light
a thousand and one shapes
water sucked into the heavens

drop deep in the mind, inner fire
cleansed and nourished

Hold purity of thought
all is peaceful
the dream a picture of psyche

ALVY CARRAGHER

Sunday Prayers

And if I speak of waiting,
then I'm speaking of the church in Gortanummera
with its sermons and communions and stained glass,
how the minutes stood still each Sunday
as I endured the ritual. A prerequisite for yoga—
hands in prayer, standing, sitting, kneeling—
a sequence that came to me without thinking.
Although, I imagine the church is abandoned now
and full of empty pews.

And if I speak of empty,
then I'm speaking of prayers about fathers and forgiveness,
despite Mary being the backbone of the rosary,
the one relatable character in the stations of the cross.
She stood before me in stone, on the left side of the church,
where only the women and children could sit.

And if I speak of that side of the church,
then I'm speaking of our hearts, slightly left of centre,
tilting our bodies back towards our mothers.

And if I speak of mothers,
then I'm speaking of mine and the silence she taught me.
Perhaps it's a trick handed down to all daughters—
how to keep words firmly under our tongues,
until they've grown long and sickening roots.

And if I speak of tongues
then I'm speaking mostly of my own,
counting the backs of my teeth
as the priest went on and on and on,
continuing his sermon until he landed
on the words he felt needed to be said.

And if I speak of words,
then I'm speaking of searching
for a place to rest my head,
where the truth will come in streams of light,
tinted red and purple and blue by stained glass,
just about vivid enough to touch.

ANNE CASEY

Suggestions for living, a cento

After Jessie Lendennie

Lay still, the sounds heard
the beginnings of comfort; feel
the sea on the wind, the fall falling
of the wave riding the horizon

and the waves recede beyond the cliffs,
beyond the trees; rows upon rows,
filling their long trailing sacks; in the darkness,
the silence at the centre of the wind, the sound of rain.

In the dark, trace a circle around the willow—
time the slowest of movements; fine rain
against thin glass, against hard stones
like so many broken children; grow

into Gypsy, Hobo, a child of rain;
know water as it seeps from sky,
from the heart; know the sharp light of sun
on bottles broken in the street.

The horizon is both this path and
the edge of the sea; and memory
is a fracturing, a breaking of light and dark
with an old dog who knows all the secret places

down the unpaved road to the calm bay;
become part of something sacred—
salmon in a small stream that rolled
down to the beach, going home or starting out.

Believe in past lives; sit and wait
for everyone to come home—
silver dogs in the sea, unhindered,
gazing down the valley to Liscannor, Lahinch

and the bay; walk the stones of Clahane:
romantic Ireland smells of soft wind;
move slowly among ghosts
whose bodies are anywhere

but here; lose place; follow another pack; maybe
take a wrong turn at the edge of the sea
as the last storm leaves again;
lay still, the night moved

past; brush wonder
as a child, fingers
tapping at windows;
reach out, softly moved.

This cento is composed entirely of lines and line segments from *Daughter and Other Poems* (Salmon Poetry, 2001) and *Walking Here* (Salmon Poetry, 2011) by Jessie Lendennie.

PAUL CASEY

Passerine

Of all the tongues I'd rather speak bird
have impulse thought and wish tuned into song
for this I'd give up every poem and word

The flummoxed squirrels think me all absurd
absorbing chorus verse refrain and idiom
but if I had my way I'd just speak bird

Throughout evolution this must have occurred
to countless sods unable to belong
who vowed surrender every poem and word

All felines I encounter over-purr
they trill insist yes something here is wrong
claws waver, cannot enter this lost bird

I should have sung the circuit I have heard
the notes deep camouflaged inside so long
when in a flash I'd give up every word

As plumage bursts through skin and senses blur
my intuition feels perfectly strong
Of all the tongues I'd far prefer speak bird
for this I'd give up every poem and word

SEAMUS CASHMAN

The Broighter Boat

i.m. Gerry O'Flaherty (d. 26/12/2019): Joycean & Dubliner

Gerry died this year on St Stephen's Day;
had a Latin mass on Monday,
was taken to the right past Mount Jerome's
Victorian chapel to a quiet corner grave,
aslant the wall. Here too cedar, cypress,
and yew commune—whisper-shade nature's nave.

We too seem votive offerings in wait,
ever eking out new boundaries to cross;
palimpsests to doubt, our inevitability
to home within earth's persistent heart
and time's bronchial lung with its secret hoards
like Broighter's treasure of La Tène art:

—tiny; in beaten gold. The boat a beauty, with mast
and yardarm, steering and companion oars,
anchor hook; forked poles; a cooking bowl
or pot for soup, libation, wine; and elegant torcs
of floral design; chain necklaces (two)
from the Middle East perhaps, or Egypt's Rome.

Like Joyce's Bloom in Dublin town, Gerry's home
and Gerry's rune; where he held close the narrative
of accident and chance encounter that illuminate
despite their missing thwarts the worlds we've bred
in plastic times. And he held true as Broighter's gold
to thought, and to its votive records of the dead.

PATRICK CHAPMAN

The Following Year

We have come again
to walk among the Turners
and you say that I look well,
that I look better
than the last time. I was mauve
and eggshell blue, a photo-
copy of myself, an impression
left out in a window for years,
a Louis le Brocquy portrait
of a shrunken Bono's head. Not
gutsy like a Bacon, no just
watery and hazy. You had
worried that my face might shed
the last of its papyrus. But
look at me now, right as rain.

This year, will we dance it instead?

The beguine through interior
twilight, from Reichenbach
to Dorset. Oh, I do love
a cataract, love a good coast.
We might catch Moriarty
tumbling from the one, splashing
down off the other. Hello,
is that Holmes? I swear I see
a Meerschaum bowl, bobbing
like a buoy. Or maybe not.

We'd best avoid the other rooms
in case of a le Brocquy.
Are you ready?
                    Let's begin.

SARAH CLANCY

Three Parishes Wait for Ophelia

Seventy seagulls or more are squatting in the lee of the wall
while curlews cry their way inland away from the coast
our seals, in closer than usual, surface and vanish
in the shallow heel of the bay, the steely grey herons
are unflappable, unperturbed by the spectacle of
a cargo ship laid up in Ballyvaughan where
the sea is a mirror and the air is lifeless and dead
there are no batteries to be had for four parishes
and there hasn't been such a run on candles
since novena season ended and the Virgin Mary statues
in Barney's cottage are abandoned in twilight
to keep their own counsel, chances are at full-tide
with the path outside flooding he heard a high-stool calling
and moved inland to Daly's to wait out the barometer,
in our house the neighbour's Jack Russell is sleeping,
her small paws twitching are the only things moving
and the dusk at New Quay and Bellharbour and Muckinish
is weighted with the baited breath of low lying places
waiting, waiting, waiting for the storm to hit,
waiting for Ophelia.

GILLIAN CLARKE

The Singer and the Song

Not chance that it's named for the salmon's way upstream,
through deeps and shallows, mountain waterfalls,
in fierce faith, love's labour, driven by dream,
pushing long nights and days against refusal.

Listening, in word and line, she heard
the too-long silenced sing their songs of truth,
her faith a stubborn force against the flood
of history to show what words are worth.

What powers such labour? Language. Poetry's spell.
The touch as you turn a page, the sound and look
of a line, its heartbeat, the call of its music,
a gleam of meaning in a glittering shoal.

All praise to word-woman's years of steady work
to set the silenced free and let them speak.

JANE CLARKE

The Lookout

Neither wind nor rain would stop him
lying in wait on the garden wall,

an hour or more, till he spotted
the yellow school bus at the top of the road.

When he heard us
laughing, shouting, squabbling,

he'd jump barking to the gravel
and run to gather his flock of five.

The evening he arrived in the kitchen
(the runt from our uncle's best collie),

he had peed on the tiles,
but never again until near the end

when his legs wouldn't carry him
to the back door, long after he'd taught us

all he knew about love
that waits in the wind and rain.

RACHEL COVENTRY

October

Let's celebrate on Friday,
let's get a takeaway coffee
and walk the prom, or
if it's raining, walk anyway,
celebrate our respective lovers
or perhaps by then, the knowledge
our hearts are still supple enough
to recover from them,
celebrate our successes
and failures, celebrate the jobs
we have and the ones we did not get
the children we put off then regretted
not having or didn't depending on the day,
the dogs who died and the one who
will sniff along beside us, busy in himself,
the parents who fucked us up entirely,
the siblings who never made sense,
let's celebrate ambitions met and those
slipping away like summer
leaving us here, shivering and alive
in the cold, sweet grip of autumn.

MAJELLA CULLINANE

Singing Lessons

I had a voice, they said. The budgerigar protested,
removed from the piano top to the next room
during lessons. I was terrified of its wings,
its beady red eyes, its ruffle of feathers.
Practising scales, I was asked if I smoked,
and if not—then why can't you hold your breath?

That would come later. If there was ever a voice,
it was marooned inside my cluttered bedroom,
far away from that teacher whose name I can't remember.
A voice that soared alone, audience of blank walls,
open windows too occupied with the street
to take any notice. I could hear myself unimpeded,

air exhaled at the right moment; the *fermata* sustained.
In any cathedral, my voice could have reached
the highest arches, the dusty motes streaming
through the stained glass windows. I'd have escaped the cage,
the budgerigar metamorphosed into nightingale.
Too bad then, I was always so terrified of heights.

ELEANOR CUMMINS

Reading on the Luas

for Jessie

You sit beside me on the Luas,
Ask, 'What's the book'?
I glance sideways,
'*Travels with Charlie.*'
You smile.
I tell you, 'It was written in 1962
But could have been written last week.'
You nod, satisfied.

You are very old, but well put together.
I imagine you have a wife
Who makes sure
You have shiny shoes,
Well-pressed trousers,
Safe. Secure.
Open to strangers on the tram.

People listened to us, curious.
We a Beckett Short,
The train sliding silently along,
Stations announced in Gaelic,
A detached, middle-class voice
Embarrassed to admit to the double Irish consciousness,
Nothing like the sounds of Connemara,
'RRRanell Aauuck, Ranelagh'.
West-Brit Dublin, with a smatter of Gaelic.

Split into those who know
On the Daniel Day Luas,
Those who don't
On the Jerry Lee Luas.
'Ah sure de Irish was bet into us,' ye say
'But,' I reply, 'Don't forget, ya sneering amadán,
First it was beaten outta yer Granny.'

Sighing into the station,
Doors glide open.
You rise, politely bow.
The conversation in my head
Between my two selves, silenced.
I nod and watch you
move on.

GERALD DAWE

Come what may

The gull-screams mean sunrise
and even though I've heard it
a hundred times before, still surprise,
somewhere between alarm and panic,

or else the soaring freewheeling bird
really hasn't a care in the world
but for this brand-new day.
Come what may, it cries, *come what may*.

MARY DORCEY

Between the Shafts

I am driven like a donkey
by my gift—
uphill and down
along rough roads and soft,
striving
with half a will
to succeed
at ordinary things,
always failing.

Drawn like a mule
hoof after head
along iron tracks
in winter,
stumbling on
the cobble-stones
tumbling into ditches.
On the cliff edge
by night
throat parched
voiceless.

Sometimes,
at the season's turn,
by a wild
mountain stream
bathing,
or it might be at dawn
breaking into
song.

On occasion perhaps
getting up a canter,
at others
a bright wind
at my back—
flying a few feet
above the crowd.

I am driven like a donkey
by my gift
along hard roads and soft,
goaded by the whip
enticed by
a sheaf of straw,
striving with half a mind
to succeed at ordinary things,
never arriving—
forever reaching.

THEO DORGAN

The Snow Farmer

The man who found himself farming snow,
his fences set out across wide pastures,
the staves dotted with crows,
was a virtuoso in this at least—
he knew that the trick lay
in sober management of the white spaces.

1989

1990

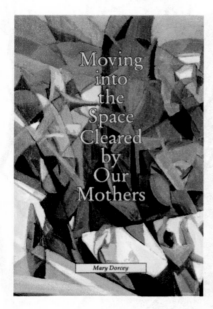

1991

1992

CAROL ANN DUFFY

Blue Dress

(Madonna del Parto, Piero Della Francesca)

It is a first time of seeing of blue, your dress.
You wear it as though you balance the bloods
                                            in your heart,
your maternity dress. Your face so solemn and sad
at the thought of the birth of God,
that the youths beside you
                              have sprouted wings of belief.
They are closing the painted curtains.

You will take off your blue, blue dress,
lie down in History's tent, and then…
But, alas, I know more than you. I wonder
if one of the youths will hang your dress
                                          from a hook
as you push and pray on the floor. Poor, gifted girl.
I would like reach out my hand
and steal your blue dress.

I think it would suit me.

SUSAN MILLAR DuMARS

Orchard, Womb, Garden

i.

orchard in the morning
calligraphy of barren trees
sky pink
snow packed high
unblemished as my mind
which has forgotten itself
I'm on my own
no footprints to follow
numb, bright
an ice child

ii.

You tell me you remember
the pain of giving birth to me.
Other mothers have forgotten
but that agony's sealed inside you
where I
used to be.

iii.

This sudden sharpness
just before sun sets
on the garden.
Shadows make richer the colours
of ashtray, bird bath, you
holding onto the back of your chair
and me. I'm here too.
Softer now than ice
my eyes wet, remembering.
It will be dark soon.

MARTINA EVANS

Barium Swallow

What was I doing there—
the family fumbler,
the dreamy one—
where every mistake
meant another spray of radiation
and doctors lashing
and bouncing?
Senior radiographers
on ten feet stilts.
In at eight a.m.
in my white uniform
my wide blue belt clasped,
shaking up the chalky
strawberry-flavoured Barium
drinks before the patient was
strapped to a table and
spun fairground-style,
the radiologist watching
the image intensifier,
tracking the passage of food,
radiographers watching
the radiologist,
the cassettes and the kilovoltage.
Turning the huge Flash Gordon dials.
Dr O'Mahoney shouting,
Drink Greedily I said!
The skeleton opened
its Halloween jaw and
I saw—not the opaque river
showing the faults
in the digestive system
twentieth-century style
but a medieval image
of the Time
that I was losing there
every day.

ELAINE FEENEY

Two-Kilometre Walk

A disused bridge climbs over
big daisies and rough wooden sleepers. I claw
upwards on hands and knees to walk the tracks,
down, down, down: where the trains
were always coming fast—

In my sleep, father gallops a bay horse
to the end of this bad land that reared
us, then made me mad: bush, orchard, famine roads:
where walking I remember my heart is made
of beating moss. My soul, thankfully regrown—

VIVIANA FIORENTINO

Shoreline

Before we turn, give me your hand.

Nothing to say
just forgetting as passers-by do.

You point the rocks that turn to North.

We guess

the whitewashed houses, the soot roofs,
Scotland over the blue, shredded in clouds, riding on a north-eastern wind.

Your palm in my palm—
a delicate whisper of lines and skin, or lands touched by your eyes.

Time rises from us—
a map of foreshores on our faces.

For we are like written letters, signs with no sounds

Listen   yet hearing them.

ANNE FITZGERALD

Eye and Ear

To Eamonn Lynskey

The ophthalmologist bids
me sit at her slit lamp

rest my chin and forehead
within its frame. She moves

in closer, shines a high
beam into darkness beyond

my cornea, not unlike torchlight
policemen shine into the back

of a refrigeration truck.
Their lux and lumens wash

over thirty-nine pairs of eyes
glistening like periwinkles

kept out of sight from Zeebrugge,
to Essex Waterglade industrial park.

The eye doctor allows yellow drops
dilate my pupils for a wider look,

tucks two thin paper tapers behind
lower lids, measures tears. Half an hour

on, eyes like bone-dry pebbles
harbour my vision where no tears flow
nor from a Monaghan driver's cargo

of hopes for a better life, frozen
to death, comes to a dead stop.

Blepharitis the ophthalmologist
blurts. Greek for eyelid, avoid hand

rubbing, spreads inflammation
as easy as traffickers seal deals

with fasting spit to open palms.
Somewhere lorries are pulling up

on laybys in sight of wildflowers
that cannot hear butterfly wings.

JOHN FITZGERALD

Magus

I would be one of the wanderers,
with heaven watching.
Observe, you reflections, I glance away.

Notice wonder spring forth its ancientness,
steep the spell held in spices, hypnotized.
In dreams I descend twenty steps at a time,

am afraid how I'll land if I fly too high.
I try not to say I, and claim myself,
a sign of consciousness uncovering.

Who calls me, from such transience?
We will ourselves into vastness,
like children at graves,

a wind with just one chance to blow,
both toward and away from itself in surprise,
or life is waste.

There are shooting stars, then that which lingers,
even hovers like a hawk, a halo.
None can bear looking straight toward the sun.

We see it reflect off the ocean by day, the moon at night.
Imagine someone's sun fly away.
What must it search for, in its burning?

Galaxies witness it bursting through silence.
May it glow to the end in spite of where it finds itself.
Let innocence cling to the universe, swirling,

get high and go hungry, distil our minds
till we can't control what pours from inside,
and at heart remain addicts, ever humble.

GABRIEL FITZMAURICE

Clown

I'm a clown, children kick me,
They see it as part of the fun,
They don't see a clown as a person,
They kick me and quickly they run

Back to the safety of ringside
Where a clown-person's hurt may not go,
The man is through with the circus.
The clown gets on with the show.

JANICE FITZPATRICK SIMMONS

Cuan Solas na Réalta

In this lockdown wish a walk
by the harbour of my heart. Magheroarty
is across the way from the solitary dock.

I walk in morning, sun just rising,
Water a dark teal in sunlight.
Sound of seabirds still. It is not quite time yet

for them to raise their varied voices;
to me a sound of yearning. I walk along
the backstrand toward the river where green

gives way to pewter. I make my way
to the bench that gives me a gallery view
of Atlantic, Ray river, and distant mountains familiar shapes.

In this version of the story it is you
who I have arranged to meet here—
conjured into taking it all in together—

the teal ocean water, the silver river
where a salmon fisherman has joined us
on the bend where ocean meets river water.
There is a glint of moving silver salmon.
I think of words never realised,
how they rise and fall, move
again to that place where they were formed.

PHILIP FRIED

To Know Thyself ...

The unquantified life is not worth living.
My pedometer tallies the 10K daily
steps I take as I strive to keep
fit in my apartment, and tracks
calories burned and food intake,
leveraging my cell phone's power.
Meanwhile my heart rate checker app
built into my fitness wearables
captures the ebb and flow of my blood,
optimizing my cardio workout.
I am known, safe, and accounted for,
and 24/7 reports on TV
update me on the virus's progress,
with morbidity and mortality
by state, and on the varying curve
whether surging up or flattening.
I circumscribe the outbreak with numbers
(though sometimes the blur of a victim's face,
suffering disease and cure,
appears atop a crumpled sheet).
Per the statistics, I'm well-briefed.

ANNE-MARIE FYFE

A Girl's Summer Bird-Journal

An off-radar snow bunting's thud makes a sudden impression on kitchen windowglass.

There's a kiwi on the shoe-polish tin we can't open. They can't fly. They say.

A honeyed light above Saint Francis haloes the non-specific songbird in *A Child's First Prayer Book*.

One day in May I'm close enough to shudder at the milky cataract on a thrush's eye.

In Primary Four we learned Odin's ravens are called *Thought & Memory*. They fly nightly across the whole known world, to bring him news of faraway places. I tell Master Connolly our birds are called *Joey & Bluey*.

A black corvid hunching his shoulders on the washing-line pole blocks the midday sun, puts the whole back lane into shadow with one flappy wingspan.

The schoolhouse-roof corncrake disappears on the day we start *Blue Book III*.

I trace the old-fashioned painstaking letters from a yellow Swan Vestas matchbox. *The Smoker's Match*.

In the end we find the panicky wren behind the shed's grass-rakes, milk-crates, paint tins, a steel tool-box.

All August I've been planning to pink-rubber-band my penpal address to the pigeon's leg once *she's on the mend*.

A kestrel swoops on our frantic border collie time after time, then soars up, & off into the blue yonder.

My mother insists it all comes down to the one & only time she neglected to greet a lone magpie outside our cemetery gates.

First a green bird, then a blue, both flown: after that I leave open the cage-door of the *little birdhouse in my soul.*

TESS GALLAGHER

River

What keeps the water from being stopped by
the rock? The rock
                        keeps stepping
                                    over it.

DAVID GARDINER

Night Reading

for Olivia & Phoebe

Awake reading
nearly all night
when you are near.

You're in my room.
I'm on the couch.
You're both under

the best blankets
I have left. Hoping
that your sleep &

my wakefulness
might mend & remember
when I'd crack doors

to the hall light
& watch you both—

mouths half open & beautiful
as only children's can

& hope one day you might know
I'm forever awake for you.

PAUL GENEGA

1984

Uptown local, 2:30 AM Sunday
Guy around my age gets on 23rd Street
Surveys empty car, sits beside me
Unsure whether to feel flattered
Or some other kind of edgy
Till he pivots winks sighs
Pulls a switchblade from his pocket
Flicks blade open, pushes it back
Into handle... flicks blade open
Pushes it in handle... all the while
Smiling queasy secret smile
Not so very different from
Man carrying a cello gets on
At Penn Station, trundles
To far end of the car, from
Bickering couple that shout
Aboard at Times Square... Mohawk
Teen with birdcage... Dietrich drag...
Him never stopping flicking
The blade smiling, flicking the blade
Smiling, when he leans over &
Announces in confidential tone
I *am Jesus... I can do anything*
I want... anything at all... & I with
Breathless effort twist lips into what
I hope passes for a non-agnostic grin
& despite stares insisting they see
Nothing from those who've joined
Our ride & despite the urge to flee
The next stop or the next, I somehow
Stay put all the way to 110th Street
Where, ungluing myself from the seat

I leave Switchblade Jesus on his eternal
Journey to the Bronx, whistle walk
Three frozen dark blocks home, roar
Of his goodbye beneath the subway grate
New York prayer stuck in my gut

DANI GILL

Crossword

I do it to reclaim your words
to gather the anagrams and
deliver them back to your hands

I can still use a pen, so I fill up the grid
and wait to hear your voice
coming from the kitchen
calling the letters, asking for the numbers

deliberating.

1993

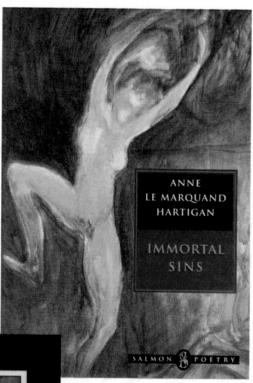

ANNE
LE MARQUAND
HARTIGAN

IMMORTAL
SINS

SALMON POETRY

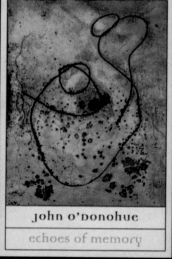

john o'donohue

echoes of memory

SALMON POETRY

1994

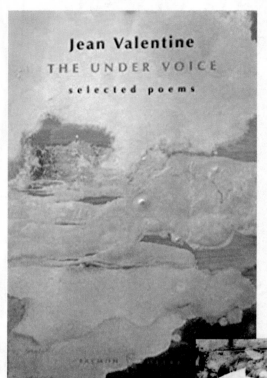

1995

1996

RICHARD W. HALPERIN

Richard Dalloway in Wisconsin

He is bringing his wife a bouquet of roses,
To tell her—he is not good with words—
That he loves her. He is walking past Lake Garth,
Across which as a boy I swam, my father

Rowing alongside me. Splinters of place,
Of time—as always with Virginia Woolf.
Mr Dalloway rushing home as St. Paul's chimes;
I buoyed up by water, love at my side

In the only way he could express it;
A marvellous university teacher—
Marlies Danziger—encouraging me
To splash around in such things.

KERRY HARDIE

World, World

for Jessie Lendennie

These days I pray to October, to light that is dying,
the last of it clinging
to leaves in the stillness, tomorrow the leaves may be gone.

I pray to the strumpet flare
of the wild cherry up on the hill,
I pray to the poplars, their soft golden leaves.

I may be gone too, no one knows, no one knows.
The world is a song that someone is singing,
but who sings the song?

Now the cherries are stretched on their rumpled bed,
the poplars have faded, the sun has lain down
on the old, heavy bones of the earth.

MAURICE HARMON

Day Care Centre

Brought by ambulance, taxi, or minibus
they enter the long room, one by one
some in wheelchairs, some on walking frames
their spirits taking the lift.
They have made it again, meet again.
They joke, spin yarns, talk of family, go back over things.
Enjoying the fun nurses go among them, ticking names
taking blood pressure, checking the pulse
arranging a doctor's visit.
Some go to the gym where they inch along
fearful and anxious gripping bars
others turn wheels, limbering up, do the bicycle jaunt
or lie back to have their legs massaged.
Here nobody raises the bar, nobody pumps iron.
It might seem they are too old or too far gone
that they ought to be back home, feet to the fire.
But no, they have left their rooms and bed-sits
fared forth at the State's expense.
Here they are equals, with dodgy tickers, lung disease
high blood pressure, shakes, spasms, dizzy spells.
No matter, this is the republic of the day care centre.
Week after week they sing the same songs
Have you ever been lonely?
Have you ever been blue?
They let it out, clap hands, release the rebel yell.
This is their day of days, their weekly come and get it.

MICHAEL HEFFERNAN

Lunch With the Hermit

I am not having any of it: what for,
where does it get me, what else can I do
to make things as they are better than they are
or were or will or can be here or there
in this or that time, take in what stride I
or my people here or hereafter may
or might be able to step up and get
the edge on for the moment as it comes
when kingfishers go up in smoke to blind
least offerings to bring my windowsills
to where I need them now or yet again
beside the if or might or anyway
as I step through my garden by the pond
to watch you turn to where I had to come?

RACHAEL HEGARTY

The Sky Road

A girl once woke up in Blytheville.
Cotton fields, lumber yards and steels mills,
but she heard Shawnee voices say *look up,*
take the sky road above Chickasawba.
She left Arkansas for Ennistymon.
Herself, the kids and the dogs, dogs galore,
walked on limestone and spied rare flowers—
cranesbill, bog orchid and mountain avens.
Yet she also caught a scent, a hunger
for books, wonderful books stuffed with poems
by folks, others with Shawnee-like voices.
So she made a home in Clare and made books.
Took some more walks, mapped the Atlantic's clouds,
nodded towards a big sky and journeyed on.

KEVIN HIGGINS

Conversation

Your shoulders fall softly
as if you're gazing down a hole
to see if you can see water
or at least the bottom of the hole
in what might be
yourself. But you can't
make it out exactly.
Perhaps you need new glasses.

Times like this you are soft
as the snail you met yesterday
while it was slithering
down your garden wall
minding its own business
and you stopped
to touch, very gently.
And it stopped
its slithering as if to say:
"Who the fuck is yer man?!"

Before going about its business
as you clicked open
the lock on the garden gate
to go about yours.

Two stones.
One male, grey, and absolute
telling the world: "Here I am.
I can take any boot put down on me."

The other so white
smooth faced
it looks almost soft.
Its hidden side ridged with complications.
If you trod on it barefoot on the beach
it could break and make you bleed.
And you'd recoil like a snail
going back into its shell.

That's the risk,
and you take it.

RITA ANN HIGGINS

My Left Hand

for Jessie

I'm writing this
with my left hand.
Not for the novelty of it
I don't give good novelty.
I'm right-handed as you know.
But some myalgia
with a squeeze of malaise
is making my right-hand go dumb.
It won't do simple things
like comb my hair
or scratch my arse
without pain.
Frankly, it's not worth the effort
so, I'm using my left hand.

Jessie Across the Years.
I know your middle name
is Across the Years.
I've seen you take off and land
in middling conditions.
You rise above territory and tenses
and words fall all around you.
I'm hiding two here
between the lines.

First word five letters.
It could work as a stand alone—
if you added an s.
It's not spank without the s,
and really let's not go there.

Second word three letters,
and it's not dog spelled backwards.
Not that you'd ever have any trouble
with dog, with or without an s.
And you'd never spank it
however bold,
leastwise that's what
I'm told.

ELEANOR HOOKER

Salire

for Jessie Lendennie

What is it we seek—
the estuary to our natal stream?
The return?
Without a mariner's compass,
sail, mast or helmsman,
we navigate by dream
and sense, by memory.
Wary of undercurrents,
of deviant tides,
we swim or die.
We leap in the Fall
against all currency.
    Salire
Cold rivers rise, restless,
as though to say—
you have come this far
but not yet arrived,
you have survived
oceans of salt,
try again, break surface here,
fresh water awaits you,
the ground is prepared.
Do it.
    Leap!
And you arrive,
swimming through
an archive of the dead—
roe to the place
of return and departure,
where the waters rhyme.

* Sailire – from the Latin, *to leap*

RON HOUCHIN

How I Met Jessie Lendennie

I was part of a workshop in Galway, Ireland in which a sweetheart of a lady, Joan McBreen, set up a reading for the participants at the Galway Arts Centre. I'd had a few poems in *Poetry Ireland Review*, so I decided to read from that issue.

After the reading, we all went round to Brennan's Yard for a drink. Soon, along with Joan walked in a woman leading two Golden Retrievers and wearing a cape—all in all Celtic goddess. Joan introduced us. Jessie said, "I liked what you read. You should send me a book manuscript sometime." I reached into my satchel, pulled out a book manuscript, and became the laughingstock of the room.

As an American, I marveled at such generosity. That was 1995, the beginning of my love affair with Salmon Publishing and the Irish land and people. I've traveled to Ireland ever since, thirty-one trips so far. And the main reason for returning so often is to visit Jessie and her family.

TIM JEANOTTE

Cuddle Dogs

Cuddle dogs look up at you
They read you, cocking their heads to
Let you know they know.

When you reach your hand out
In the dark
A cuddle dog will be there
A warm weight beside you.

Cuddle dogs start out fast
Running rings around you
Then they slow down,
As you've had to.

Padding along at your side
Or a little ahead.
Turning and looking
To check you're still there.

FRED JOHNSTON

Mascara Wine

'*Heureux qui, comme Ulysse, a fait un beau voyage*'
—Joachim du Bellay, 1522-1560

The wine of Mascara was our *grand cru*
A hardy, totalitarian little wine sharp on the nose
And easy to swallow—

We smuggled it by the car boot-load from where
It was legal to where it was not,
Where it was twice the price in back alleys.

We drank to Africa and smoked grass
Around tables set and loaded with French bread
Under balcony skies clear and brutal as mirrors.

Drunk, hysterical, homesick, we heard
The first prayer-call and the sound of light
Breaking on the hills like surf on a beach

We the conquerors, the teachers, sucking
On the lips of parched wine bottles
Prickling with the first sweat of the new day

To stink under single bed-sheets and imagine
Our own death, to walk about naked in raping heat
Humming like wires tightening on every breath

On the edge of tears and apology—
On the edge of a desert, its elemental emptiness
Fixing its teeth into our crackling bone:

The wine of Mascara was our *grand cru*
A hardy, totalitarian little wine sharp on the nose
And easy to swallow.

JEAN KAVANAGH

Constanse's Ladder

*(In collaboration with the Norwegian artist
Cathrine Constanse Gjelsnes)*

Her *Sculpture in Context* hangs
under a high skylight of glass
in the Gallery of Art at Kunstnernes Hus;
a rope-ladder, with rolling-pins for rungs,
donated and collected
from old Norwegian kitchens.

How does a *hussy* dare to climb
up horizontal years
of housewives' shaping,
kneading, folding, over daily tasks,
over sweat and aprons,
over pride and fuss
saved for special occasions,
over every woman's
wooden weapon?

Let's look up, keep lookout
in this formal space, leap over
the museum barrier ropes,
kick off our shoes,
place our bare toes
where calloused hands
rolled out their lives;
we can only rise
on an idea,
ascend above
the stories of the hearth,

find a soaring voice
between the sway
of song, up beyond
words of lost librettos
for the music
of Nannerl.

The poetry of imagining
makes light of female feet,
impossible, as
a salmon's leap upstream;
up we roll,
grandmothers, teaching mothers,
teaching daughters, up,
umbilical with hope.

COLM KEEGAN

Cill Rialaig Haiku

The threat of a Ram
Two old stares lock horns
He turns before me

I follow through fence
Sound of ocean chewing earth
The call of the edge

Lying starfish flat
I stick out my neck
Eyes fall into sea

Stark white of sheep's bone
Blown clean by Atlantic breeze
Not the only one

Shape etched from cliff face
giant dog trying to catch breath
The sea won't relent

Pursued by five sheep
As if I am their Shepherd
Don't look at me

Can't find a through-line
Something about the landscape
Makes this the best way

Surprise from the high stile
This is a peninsula
New wind in my face

Ruined barracks on top
Even empty space up here
Was taken from us

1997

The
Shadow
Keeper

Jean O'Brien

Unlegendary Heroes
Mary O'Donnell

Salmonpoetry

1998

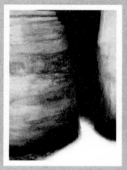

THE WHITE PAGE
An Bhileog Bhán
Twentieth-Century Irish Women Poets

Joan McBreen

salmonpublishing

1999

2000

The Salmon Carol Ann Duffy
poems selected and new 1985 – 1999

salmonpoetry

DES KENNY

An Iconic Moment in a Bookshop

On a bright summer's day, sometime during the early 1980s, the door of the shop opened suddenly and this extraordinary lady made a grand entrance. Mother was standing at the end of the counter, as if by appointment, and solemnly welcomed the lady as she would royalty.

A short and polite conversation ensued during the course of which a palpable and growing sense of excitement became more and more evident. As this excitement reached its zenith, the lady suddenly produced what looked like a sheaf of paper and, with great ceremony presented it to mother with the words: "Mrs Kenny, this is just the beginning".

Although there were just a few people present, this was indeed a momentous moment. The lady, Jessie Lendennie, presented my mother with the first issue of a new journal "The Salmon, a journal of poetry and prose, as an alternative voice in Irish Literature". A brand new era of indigenous creative literature in Galway had begun.

The whole episode lasted less than five minutes but after nearly sixty years of bookselling, it remains one of those iconic moments that a Bookseller never forgets. While it was happening a sharp image of Sylvia Beach and Adrienne Monnier jumped to mind for the simple reason that they were two women with bookshops in Paris who also broke the mould. As always happens on occasions like this, nobody noticed and life on High Street went on as normal.

Now, some forty years later, while the journal no longer exists, the Salmon Press and Bookshop are alive and kicking. After what now seems a short period of time, it began to publish books of poetry written mainly by women and poets such as Rita Ann Higgins, Mary O'Malley, Eva Bourke, Moya Cannon and the late gentle Anne Kennedy became household names.

Although it seemed at first that the poets published by Salmon were exclusively female, Lendennie had a wider vision and books written by such poets as Gabriel Fitzmaurice, Michael Gorman, Seamus Cashman, Michael D. Higgins, Fred Johnston and Kevin Higgins appeared. In addition, the Press had a healthy international catalogue.

It wasn't always easy. There were times when there was hardly a crust on the table. This did not deter our Jessie and when in 2007 she published an anthology—26 years after she walked in the door of the bookshop—entitled *Salmon: A Journey in Poetry 1981–2007*, it had contributions from 106 poets, who knew what they were about. Now some forty years after she said to my mother, "Mrs Kenny, this is just the beginning", we now know she meant it.

Jessie Lendennie, Lady, Poet, Publisher Extraordinaire, we salute you.

BRIAN KIRK

Small Things

for Catherine Corless

She wraps a stone in an old sweet paper, just like she's seen
the older girls do, offers it to a streel of a thing from the home,
watching big eyes light up for a moment before going out.

The girl was famished; what if she'd put it in her mouth?
Some say a stone sucked from time to time, will trick
the stomach into thinking it's being fed, releasing enzymes

to work on what's not there, adding a peculiar ache
to habitual hunger pangs. She often thinks of it, that meanness,
a small thing that stays with her, won't let her be. Just leave it alone,

that's what some people said, why go upsetting the holy nuns?
Even after she counted them out, painstakingly adding new names
to the list of dead babies, the causes of death: measles, TB,

hunger, pneumonia, neglect. Four euro for a certificate,
paid out of her own pocket, the only proof they once lived.
Now dead. Small lives that nobody noticed or cared about,

small deaths that deserved no more than the stroke of a pen.
Not the word of a priest, a sad song from a choir, a slow walk
to a grave where earth falling on oak could be the final, solemn

sound before the tears of loved ones filled the air and soft words
telling the story of little him or her and what they liked or hated, or how
they smiled when the gardener's dog chased pigeons from the seeded

rows in Spring, or how the tiny fingers curled about the handle of a spoon at supper time, or how their shiny cheeks went dipping in cold water at Halloween, russet as the apples in the bowl. Small things I know.

She found their names and gave them back to us although we weren't sure, surprised to find we needed them as much as they had needed us back then. Each one so small, a tiny gift, a question asked and answered with her love.

JOSEPH LENNON

Aftersong

Time has went, time beyond,
Love has sung, so and on.

Mountains through windows,
Days are spent, lived no matter,

Mountains of butter, curling
In the hotel, silks of songs curtailed,

A dog wags through the room,
Bringing the must of rain with him,

A dummy piano, far from tuned
Sits in the foyer, painted shut

Yet opens by the gingery
Fingers of boys, reviving

Unmoored promises
Of lovers, of keys, of hours like this.

Time has went, time beyond,
Love so sings, on and on.

Kenmare, 2018

RAINA J. LEÓN

i have bought

all the little gems to make the prison palatable   casita for the back
yard with the make-believe grill and the little seat next to it curved
into plastic   a slide he cannot climb without my achy hands
to help   an easel and a mound of chalk for him to create punk
graffiti of two   all the pots filled with victory   gardens
he learns to water with a steady hose   mint mountain
tender ají dulce   potato fronds poisonous in their flowering
zucchini and fig and hyssop and chamomile   watermelon
and honeydew and kale and radish   we tend the tender
green pluck and smell and taste   in the front yard a picnic table
and a child-sized adirondack chair where he sits these mother eyes
always adoring him   he picks his blues and cherries   eats
them glossed in dirt while he watches the masked and unmasked
pass by   sometimes he greets them in time
sometimes they are already a half block away before the ciao and
tentative wave   he studies all who pass   our vibrant garden
lemon in its slow turn from hard green orb to bright and fleshy
yellow   the butterfly and bees cavort a small entertainment
compared to the study of humanity close and yet far   how
much have i spent on the trinkets   i don't count   won't   the
practice softens   *we cannot run together or be together*   we
avoid walking by nearby parks   he cries to play   the ache
burns   and so i dream of another activity   i buy the things
and invent games with things we have   pots and pans
cardboard boxes to climb and paint and trample in the hopes of
riches and that the memories of this time   will be of joy   this
is mothering   my pernicious love   how i think on those
who have loved me   loved my hands to shape this softness
wonder the folds of them in thumb swirls and life lines

MICHAEL LONGLEY

Embroidery

Can you imagine Mary McDiarmid
Selecting silks from her work-basket
And embroidering for you by lamplight
Tablecloths, napkins, dressing-table
Sets, cushion covers, dolls' dresses
With her own designs—marigolds,
Roses, hollyhocks, lupins, violets,
Michaelmas daisies—flowers and buds
In abstract herbaceous borders,
Stem stitch, satin stitch, feather stitch,
Stitches that never come undone,
And for their protection over time
Gathering up within the hoop
All her great-great-grandchildren?

VICTOR LUFTIG

In the splinters of the thunderbolt[1]

In a film from the National Library of Ireland's celebrated Yeats exhibition, Seamus Heaney speaks with respect and evident empathy for Yeats's public eccentricities: "If I met him, I don't know what I would feel. I might have felt, 'Oh come off it, Willie.' But on the other hand, I know a few people with affectations, and the older I get the more I admire them, because they're a way of retaining privacy and inner freedom, you know?"[2] I think we should take Jessie Lendennie's persona—at least from when I knew her best, in Salmon's early days—just as seriously: we should think of what defenses a single American woman in 1980s Ireland might have needed, especially one who was challenging entrenched notions of what might count as an Irish lyric and its under-writing Irish self. I realize now how much I misunderstood what seemed to me excessive. It seems to me no more than what was necessary to sustain a press that could not possibly then have been projected to last this long, let alone to thrive.

Jessie Lendennie came to visit the university where I was teaching during the spring of 1989. Much work my former students have contributed—in their published scholarship, in their getting important work broadcast or reprinted, etc—has followed from that visit, as has much of what has been happiest and most satisfying about my own life and work. The principles of inclusiveness she introduced us to and attached Salmon to are no less urgent now. And the greatness of the body of poems she has put into print that might never have been published otherwise makes her worthy of consideration alongside great enabling figures of twentieth century literary history such as Maxwell Perkins, Alain Locke, and Carmen Callil.

The volume that I've always thought of as epitomizing Salmon's contribution is *Two Women, Two Shores*, partly because I greatly admire the poems by Medbh McGuckian and Nuala Archer printed there and partly because the dialogue it represents seems to me both so important and, in terms of the vehicles available in Ireland at the time, so unlikely to have been given a forum.[3] How many conventions had to be flaunted to bring together that pairing? To make great, inclusive things happen in art, in Ireland or anywhere, has always required some suggestion of lunacy. 'Crazy like a fox,' I hear people say sometimes; but lest that fox here suggest Yeats's belated absent sweeper, I prefer comparison to our Yank symbol of nobility, dignity, and daring: Crazy like an eagle.

VICTOR LUFTIG
University of Virginia

NOTES

[1] From Robinson Jeffers, "The Beaks of Eagles," https://allpoetry.com/The-Beaks-Of-Eagles

[2] "The Mask: Yeats, the Public Man," Yeats, The Four Films, National Library of Ireland, 2006

[3] But it's appropriate that this current volume is edited by Alan Hayes from Arlen House, another such essential vehicle. How much subsequent history, including Salmon's, follows, for instance, from *In Her Own Image* by Eavan Boland, a key advocate for Salmon and Jessie, who'd surely have wanted to be part of this book?

PHIL LYNCH

Words Play

My words are wagging their tails,
long hanging tongues
laughing at the world,
pleased to be playing games,
chasing shadows, straining leads,
noses poking into all sorts,
leaving marks;
ears perked
to detect the slightest
nuance in sound,
bark at the ready
beware of the bite.

THOMAS LYNCH

Who's Counting?

for Jessie Lendennie, Editrix & Publisher

It's more than thirty some odd years now, Jessie
since dozing on your sofa in the Claddagh—
that low ceilinged stone manse, ever a frenzy
like a river run of spawning salmon,
mad anxious to replicate Creation,
something out of nothing, as with magic,
a rabbit yanked from out the empty hat,
the disappearing coin that reappears,
the queen of hearts in the suspicious deck,
the gypsy beauty sawed it seems in half:
just so your bringing Salmon Poetry
into being on a shoestring and dream.
You haven't yet awakened from it Jess,
forty years gone blurring by. Who's counting?

JOAN McBREEN

Ten Chestnut Trees in Letterfrack

O chestnut tree, great rooted blossomer,
Are you the leaf, the blossom or the bole?

'Among School Children', W.B. Yeats,
1928

Every spring, flowers in bloom
lean into the rain;
crocus, hyacinth, tulips,
with their secret centres
open in the gales.

When boys glanced out
dormitory windows at chestnut trees
it was unlikely their secrets
were shared with tree after leafless
chestnut tree, all ten of them—

a barricade, a wall from the village
of Letterfrack, from mountains
in every season, from lost homes,
towns, cities, that would exist
for them no more.

In February, the leafless trees
are settled in their regime
of standing guard over,
and between, inhumanity
as the boys knew it—

Never the possibility of love.
What was it? Who did it belong to?

Never to reach them
through locked doors, windows—
not to touch again a mother
or a father's hand held out,
never to know chestnut blossoms—

only those rarely placed in time
on unmarked graves
of the children who died.

O Letterfrack. Let your spring wind
rustle and move the young leaves
when they appear
and catch our eyes in tree
by tree, as we shiver and weep.

THOMAS McCARTHY

Butterfly Summer

It was while placing a slab of old red sandstone at my uncle's feet
That I saw, hovering over a blaze of furze, the three rare species

Of blue butterfly, the silver-studded blue, the chalkhill blue,
And the brown argus with its blue fuselage. We took the summer off

To find the little skipper on a clump of tor grass. With luck, you said,
We're sure to find as well the delicate wood white, the Essex skipper,

And its English friend, the clouded yellow. Rare enough they were
Among a million wings of painted ladies. Over fifty species

We found that summer, migrants and stay-at-homes, fellows
Who might hop over to Ireland to say a brief hello, blown off the Irish Sea

Onto a picnic table at Enniskerry or Ireland's Eye. It was when we were down
To the last three butterflies of the British land-mass that you broke away,

Without as much as a parting drink or a midnight argument.
I sat in the tent we stole from Canon Mahon, I sulked because I knew

The luck you'd have once you went down to the sea, the luck
You've always had in your seafaring, seeing mermaids and dolphins

Off the Azores, hearing the lost cry of the Maid of Inchydoney
As you rounded the Fastnet, seeing Peig's lost child playing with seals

As you entered the Blasket Sound, I thought, my God, what luck—
Sure enough, as you rose from your berth to brew your liquorice-thick

Greek coffee they fell out of the sky into your salty palm;
The silver-spotted skipper, the Scotch argus and the brown hairstreak.

I agree it was the best time of year to see such butterflies, but, for
God's sake, your brief time on the Solent, your coordinates, your luck.

AFRIC McGLINCHEY

Chaos and Creation

The horizon is both this path
and the edge of the sea

Jessie Lendennie

Begin with dogs in a boat,
dogs in the snow,
an open trunk and a laughing dog.
Begin with stone walls, a bog, an ocean.
Begin with dogs as an opera,
like sonata rain on the pavements.
Begin with a song and epiphany:
that freedom comes from resistance.

Begin with a promise,
a flung-open door, a fine line.
Begin with a series of insights,
like the dots-and-dashes of fireflies.
Begin with the wild Atlantic,
and vocals, maracas, nuances.
Begin with a killer hook
and end with the bright of surprises.

MEDBH McGUCKIAN

The Thankless Paths to Freedom

In the dry summer of 1950,
I became accustomed to seeing the field,
Promising the eye a natural step.
We no longer see it well.

When I drive by the field,
What I see is different from what I imagine,
The makings of an answer
Where I ask all night.

The field retained our shapes,
Sometimes softened by snow. I am reminded
Every year of these workings
Of the field, its gypsiness.

Its colours varied with the time of day,
A piece of yellow taffeta to be worn
Above the heart and blend so well
With the dead leaves.

A flowing curtain, a ruffled tablecloth,
A glass bed with glass sheets,
Brown cedar parlour
In a sea of claret and blue,

An otherwise uninvited black,
The jade snow and sky-view factor
Of the flat cemetery. The air
Entrapped in the ice-core

Of the light-demanding tree
Forced it into the city
Which might have been a text
That no-one would ever read.

From where we're sitting
On the shoulders of Ireland,
The towering stack of pallets
For the bonfire has grown significantly in size.

(The urge to festivalize).
This braille has vanished,
This pixilated kiss, the rib-like shadows
Clogging the low-lit corridors of The Maze.

For such a word is badly wanted,
Like the soundwalk I took
With a woman angel, to lift these sounds
Found in the English of my mind.

Our friendship might have skated
But something will die in me which is meant
To be immortal, unless I go back, do nothing
But breathe, above the city dust line.

ETHNA McKIERNAN

Light Rolling Slowly Backward

It's August, the season of regret,
the season of late beauty brittling
on the edge, months before
the frost. Crickets drone
their low nighttime hum

and sadness passes like a light
wind through the windows.
What is it that we miss?
The lilies are long gone, but phlox blooms
deep pink and cosmos sway
their bright yellow hearts out.

It's August and we're hurtling
toward November, even as
the glory burst of Fall color lies ahead.
Light rolls slowly backward now
while days shorten. Our shadows grow.

In high school, I remember memorizing
Margaret, are you grieving
over Goldengrove unleaving?

That must be what this mourning is,
days away from what's to come,
even as the crickets chirr
their bright summer song.

Love, if I knew you, ever found you—

2001

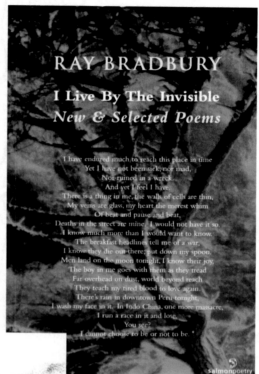

RAY BRADBURY

I Live By The Invisible
New & Selected Poems

I have endured much, to reach this place in time
Yet I have not been sick, nor mad,
Nor ruined in a wreck,
And yet I feel I have.
There is a thing in me, the walls of cells are thin,
My veins are glass, my heart the merest whim
Of beat and pause and beat,
Deaths in the street are mine, I would not have it so.
I know much more than I would want to know.
The breakfast headlines tell me of a war,
I know they die out there; put down my spoon,
Men land on the moon tonight, I know their joy,
The boy in me goes with them as they tread
Far overhead on dust, world beyond reach
They teach my tired blood to love again.
There's rain in downtown Peru tonight,
I wash my face in it. In Indo China, one more massacre,
I run a race in it and lose.
You see?
I cannot choose to be or not to be. "

salmonpoetry

In the Chair
Interviews with Poets from the North of Ireland

2002

John Brown

salmonpublishing

The Separation of Grey Clouds
MICHEÁL FANNING

2003

2004

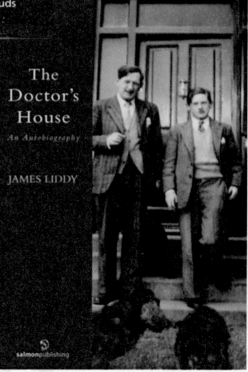

The
Doctor's
House
An Autobiography

JAMES LIDDY

salmonpublishing

DEVON McNAMARA

Prints

for Jessie

There is this walking
barefoot
through Security
into the bell of blue
as if you left a trail of whorls
over the sweep of sea, as if
starlings in dark clouds tilting
tipped the cradling moon
and suddenly you're walking
on a quiet curve of road
to that pub in Kilshanny.

August
crumbs of scones
your fluttering pages.
The little rambler rose
is listening
to flights of words, their anguishes
their silences and loves
and to your five dog shuffle
        out there in the car, spent
        and wet from the shine of the Bay.

And there's another walking of the earth's wild songs round
her four corners over widening waters rising, when cheeky winds
puff aloft old maps and parchments, airline tickets, raging empty
sleeves of clouds, and smoky cobalt thunderheads rough up island
nations, shipping lanes, and all the desperate launchings, rainbow
of oil on the slicked sand where the gull stands
baffled.

Still, when the old maple tree came down
in the storm, the sweet air found again
the shoe of the plough horse
and rejoiced.

They'd marked the wagon road
with what their working animal wore
out, and then the iron sank a century,
type of one tender mud shagged foot.

You see him walk his furrows in his harnesses,
feel how sleeping in his stall in the bank barn down
where the big sandstones still rest in earth, he dreams
another walking of the sun, his feet unshod alive
in the field
where you walk too
in the long grass
shining
and you speak
to him.

MARY MADEC

A Burren Fractal

i.m. Tim Robinson 1935–2020

I learned how to make *the good step*
on the earth, as you said,
my foot an imprint of care, an embrace.

I listened to the world grow
with the rising of the light
and as the light was rising, you died.

Now is the time of the knapweed,
field scabious and sweet marjoram,
the world turning relentlessly,

the height of summer gone,
winter soon to come
and in some graveyard far away

you are softening into the earth.
I can hear you say
it's where you belong.

I look out over warm limestone
to the islands you mapped,
I am taking each day, rapt, one step at a time.

NOTE:
Tim Robinson was an English writer and cartographer, famous
for his maps and books on the Aran Islands, Connemara and the
Burren in Ireland. He died from Covid 19 on April 3rd, 2020.

MÁIGHRÉAD MEDBH

Vagrant

A tall man habitually pulling a wheeled case must soon
grow crooked as a crane. Trundling by the parked cars
on Richmond Road he's already curtailed by his mode.
For this calling small and stocky might be a better suit
but most I see this week are lanky, made for sidling past
and between crowd snags, not folding into sepia alleys
or stretching across doorways their full length exceeds.

I think of long-distance runners perennially pinched.
Bony we say though it's not the bone. It's the revelation.
Framework pushing to the fore. We'd prefer a border
of soft pulp, the feel of it, to the uneasy disciplined rind.
I imagine he follows tracks—task and thought one path—
that birdish compulsion of the head bent on spotting
movements, homing on the complicated flicker of food.

He pulls two black cases and a leather satchel. His English
is poor so where will he stop. Back in his pulverised city
there are rooms under too much dispute and no parent
left to redeem them. Neighbours came at him screeching
over tiny misdoings. An immense concourse of pale-green
scales and fan-speedy wings occupied the street, pressing
in on his steps. A full scale many pronged ignorant attack.

Urban air at night is porous. I like it better too. Its sweat
disparately spread, becoming fainter scent. More subtle
entities eke out: aqueous infractions; palpable frettings.
Worse-off comrades and renegades with knives are cruxes
with recognisable codes. Gutter-curses, fire-scars, drug-
trawls desperate or lethal, are anyway discernible as solid
acts. You die live and bemaim all at once, the hero's way.

His face sags and he smells of crevices. Another corridor
he'd pass for professor. Wide intense brow. Purposed walk.
He perturbs the library staff. Is there anyone they can ring.
They're blank as a planned re-zoning. They speak the word
Intervention. They ponder it as their grandparents did
the fire built by a human emeritus in return for a small
plate and a cup of trot-a-mouse tea. It's not what it means.

PAULA MEEHAN

One Dog Singing

I admire Jessie Lendennie for many things: for her own work; for founding a poetry press on the very edge of Europe; for first bringing into print poets numbered amongst the finest of my generation; for facilitating my cross-Atlantic life-long friendship with poets who found a home in Salmon's list, Ron Houchin, Art Stringer, Kathryn Kirkpatrick, David Gardiner; for her taste in shoes; for her love of dogs.

Jessie edited and published *Dogs Singing: A Tribute Anthology* ten years ago and included two poems from this household, both written about our dog Bella, my own 'Who'd Be A Dog?' and Theo Dorgan's 'Night Walk with Bella'.

When Bella, who is a pup forever in my poem, was dying, I rang the vet to ask about coming to the house and euthanasing her and he talked me through the process. And he talked me through the costs. All very expensive: fanciest was a real wooden box with a brass nameplate, a slot covered in transparent plastic where a picture of the beloved pet could be placed and a guarantee that the ashes within, packaged in handmade paper, were hers alone; next was a plastic bronze-effect urn with a brass-effect nameplate and the ashes within in handmade paper; and finally the budget option, the one I went for, a cardboard tube with the ashes within in a plastic bag.

Bella had been the most amazing dog. A collie lab cross with a dash of retriever in the gene mix, daughter of a working cattle dog from north county Dublin. When I phoned to ask about getting one of the litter I was told they were all gone except for the 'runt'. Turns out Bella had been the only bitch in the litter and that determined that she was designated the runt. All the males were already taken. I don't know whether it was indignation on behalf of bitches everywhere or intuition that had me say, sight unseen,

'I'll have her', but a few hours later we were standing in the farmyard and taking into our arms her black furriness.

Adored by family, friends, neighbours, she had her own active social life & everywhere we went she was greeted with smiles, petting and delight. She would lie on her back and sing long involved hymns to those humans she was especially devoted to.

She was totally blind for the last year of her life & I became her seeing eye human. She retrained to a whole new set of instructions, at thirteen disproving the old saw that you can't teach an old dog new tricks. She was diagnosed with an auto immune syndrome and we were referred to a specialist veterinarian eye doctor who turned out to be Bono's vet, charging Bono prices. He didn't offer any hope, the failing eyes were an element in a larger process of degeneration. We understood she was running out of time. We tried everything to extend her spell with us but eventually faced the inevitable.

The day came and the vet and a nurse arrived to give Bella the shot. Theo and myself held her, all three of us lying out on her paw print rug. She died in our arms, her great devoted heart slowing to a stop. I was distraught. As they carried her body out to their car I grabbed up Jessie Lendennie's *Dogs Singing*, that big hefty anthology of human devotion to our four pawed pals, and sobbing and spluttering announced 'Bella is a celebrity dog. There are two poems about her in this book!' I insisted they take the anthology. They were nonplussed but no doubt used to erratic utterance and gesture from grieving dog owners.

Months went by & I eventually stopped into the vets to collect Bella's ashes, expecting to be handed a cardboard tube, the budget option. When the vet came from the storeroom with the wooden box, with the brass nameplate & the slot for the photograph I thought there had been a terrible & pricy mistake.

'No extra charge', he said. 'Sure isn't she a celebrity dog'.

CHRISTOPHER MERRILL

Derecho

The song of the authoritarians
Begins with threshers separating the wheat
From the chaff, in a season of death and disease,
As a derecho sweeps across the prairie,
Uprooting trees, flattening towns and cities,
Distracting everyone from the corruption
Endemic to a failing government.

———————

Gustavus Detlef Hinrichs was the chemist
Who identified the prairie hurricane,
The straight-line storm phenomenon he named
Derecho, from the Spanish adjective
For direct—as in the political
Maneuvers some will undertake to ruin
The institutions of democracy.

———————

When the Marine band plays "Hail to the Chief,"
The guests salute the owner of the club,
Who seems determined to destroy the country
He claims to love. See how he hugs the flag
Like a contestant in a beauty pageant.
The guests applaud him calling journalists
Enemies of the state. A storm is brewing.

GERALDINE MITCHELL

Bedroom Ghazal

Rain needles the window like hail across the bedroom,
  drives sharpened points hobnail across the bedroom.

A single thrush stakes out the dawn with song,
  strings ribbons through the air that sail across the bedroom.

Of all rooms in the house this holds most mystery,
  No Entry in bold letters nailed across the bedroom.

Secrets slip between plump pillows, sealed or shared,
  or open with intent, tell-tale across the bedroom.

Burning with remorse a woman watches
  her lover's puckered face, pale across the bedroom.

O bring back peace to this most sacred place where love
  like orchids must be tended, frail across the bedroom.

KELLY MOFFETT

Dear Jessie

This morning in Kentucky I knelt down to a snail as small as a semicolon
and traced the trail of slime it made on the sidewalk almost silver

in the morning light and as straight as this line and remembered
the snails of Ennistymon. There are 150 types of snails in Ireland

but I saw them one at a time: the swirl of yellow and brown, each
shell larger than a crow's egg. You may have come from America,

but in the Burren with the lichen and grikes and the low clouds and sea,
you have become your landscape. I see you as a cliff side, a hermit's

rock cave, the rough current and sometimes as a single sentence,
soaking as a teabag in the horizon. You preserve us. Sew each word

to a page. There are 1,165 species of lichen in Ireland. I remember one,
bright red in a dip of limestone. Shannon lapping up the afternoon rain

that had pooled there. The reflection of her nose meeting her actual nose.
And I thought of all the reflections you've photographed in the River Inagh

wondering what you see in each one: a memory or a mood or another kind
of language. My hand feeling a nettle's sting for the first time, I watched

your bear figurines lumber across the mantle in your office and I stared
at the peat in the hearth and thought of you as one of those bears. There

are six common types of rock in Ireland and I believe over time I have
carried all of them home. Wanting to take something back, Ireland,

the landscape, or what I have come to know as you.

NOEL MONAHAN

Journey Upstream

for Jessie Lendennie, founder of Salmon Poetry

Never one for fad, fame and fashion,
You held your finger on the pulse of time,
Sniffed out the magic of verse
At home in your Zach and Zookie world
Of *Singing Dogs*
                    You created a new myth:
Reconnected us with the Salmon
Brought us back in time to
Mountain berries dropping into a well
Where Finn the boy burnt his thumb
Sucked it better and solved the mystery
Of the journey of souls, journey of salmon,
Journey of going home with an inimitable
Jessie Lendennie chuckle.

ALAN JUDE MOORE

To Peacefully Conquer the World

(from the family history of Alexander & Dimitri Moore)

In the city of New York in 1851
Isaac Singer established his firm
and began the process of patenting
straight needled sewing machines
(being as they were an improvement
on the previous way of doing things)

We all begin in some way similar:
through desert treks or clinging to vines
we arrive on islands, inlets and coastlines
construct our huts and hunker down
pretend to be natives of some place

So in an 1851 of European upheaval
Peterburgsky Station opened in Moscow
after a while becomes Nikolayevsky
(named for a Tsar of course
who cared very little for the transport of plebs
between the first city of his Empire and the second)

It was renamed again (as is the way
when you get to naming things
after the power of people over other people)
Oktabyrsky, and then
when a man needed to be reminded
where he was really going
they named it Leningradsky

The Prussians around this time opened up their Ostbahn
from Berlin to Gdansk and on to Kaliningrad
(In 1851 probing the Soviet borders)

In Hyde Park enterprising Victorians built a crystal palace
and at *The Great Exhibition of the Works of the Industry of all the Nations*
displayed selections of faux Irish jewellery
in the Celtic Revival style that was fashionable at the time—
(the Irish bourgeoisie believing
they were mostly descended from kings)

Anyway, a brooch that had been buried beneath the muck of Meath
for a thousand years was found by a peasant woman
They cleaned it up and named it after royalty
(As we know by now, that's the way with these things)

As for us
your antecedents of course were scattered still
finding places, still making their way
from Halberstadt, Galway, Astrakhan and Naples

except in Dublin in 1851 our namesakes
wake onto streets that have folded since back into the city

and from tenement windows in the North Dock ward
they stare at the skeletons coming forth

and curse them for having lived

SINÉAD MORRISSEY

Four Zero

after Thomas Tallis, 'Spem in Alium'

A present for Elizabeth on her birthday: hope
looped out like chiffon silk from a voice in
lonely proclamation, urging any
with a heart to be lifted—*Come!*—& other
voices, one for each year of Her life, who have
hearts for hope, who've listened, answering *I*
in turn, so that none is outlawed, none
is left adrift on the singing balconies, not threaded in. O

Our Humility!   Henry razed a village so his lord-
ly Nonsuch Palace might be raised to house a Queen, but
the ghosts of the lost come back, they clamber in
through holes in the fretwork, rents in the tapestries, *my*,
they mouth, appalling faces lit with fellow-
envy as they swell. If palaces are ships these are Her passengers.

JOHN MURPHY

Daughter

There are stones on the rough track home
sharp enough to hurt your tender feet,
and if you look for it, a hard turning that's yours to find
with just enough give for all that you can take.

But today the midday sun is warm on your back,
and yesterday's rainstorm is forgotten.
As for tomorrow, it's just that noisy wind
that never blows.

And happiness is a child walking
with you through the wildflowers
whose common names you know,
a harvest never reaped, never sown.

JOAN NEWMANN

What Does Your Head Weigh?

The boy on the check-out tells me
that his mother says
a human head is the weight
of a bowl on a bowling green
and that is why
pillows indent, don't last
past a year—our dense heads
compressing the stuffing.

Because he looks as if
he feels foolish for this engagement
I say, with surprise,
I didn't know that.

*My mother says you should
replace them every year,
not wait 'til they are flat.*

*Oh dear, I think most of our pillows
are flat. That is good to know,*
as I receive my change.

What on earth had made him think of pillows?
What on earth had made him tell me?
I was buying a cauliflower
and a jar of chickpeas.
No trigger there, then.
Maybe the cauliflower, though, brain-like.

The boy and the bowls
and the weight of the human head
and the pillows, ghost his till.

He doesn't work there anymore.

Sometimes I think of him (and his mother)
when I lay my big, heavy head
on my flat pillow.

EILÉAN Ní CHUILLEANÁIN

In Ostia, August 2020

My first night in Italy since the whole world changed—
and what has changed? The taxi-driver overcharges,
he drives me past the ruins of the port, and the Papal tower,
to the hotel where they remember me
but also, as before, think I am German—
because of my hair? Because I am old and travelling alone?
There is food, and a glass, and I am alone
on the warm terrace looking out
on the small pool and the sunset. As before,
a cat appears exactly as the sun goes down,
and a kind of mechanical crab
with a long flex that arches like a snake swimming
begins to crawl around the bottom of the pool,
bangs its nose off the tiles, recoils and begins again.

2005

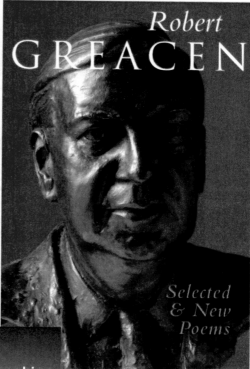

2006

In Daily Accord
FRANK GOLDEN

2007

2008

Signs, Translations
John Hildebidle

KERRIE O'BRIEN

Clearing

And isn't it what we all look for

That place

Where you can kneel against the earth
And its knowing

Times
When all we want is quiet
And an answer

Always easier in hindsight

To see
How the dots joined

How the path
Was rose strewn,
Lit by stars

All laid out
Just right for you.

CLAIRR O'CONNOR

Withheld

I pretend disinterest
in company with those
I'm afraid to trust,
no longer chat
with the groups
of young women
at the communal
stairwell. Their
laughter numbs
me. I want
to be swallowed
by love. The only
voice I need is yours.
Fatigue, lost vision
day and night.
So many
disappeared.
Dead bodies
in the street
rubble.
The revolution
has been
renamed.
The young
fall silent.

EDWARD O'DWYER

All The Courage I Had

for Knute Skinner

I saw her up ahead.
I was certain it was her,
though she was walking
with her back to me, the hood
of her raincoat over her head.

I called up all the courage I had
just to ask her. I even called up
the courage I didn't know I had,
because I was going to need
it all, every last drop.

She didn't seem overly...
Well, overly anything, if you must know.
I was a car that turned up
and pulled in to the side of the road
when the rain was coming down,

a car facing in the right direction.
I would do until I didn't do,
that was the impression,
but yes is also yes—you just have
to tell yourself that sometimes.

She wasn't saying much,
nor was I saying much.
I'd used up all the courage I had,
every last drop, by that point.

JANE O'HANLON

A Door into the Light

'*As someone "involved in the poetry thing" for years, as poet, editor, reviewer and one-time board member of Poetry Ireland, the long endurance of Jessie Lendennie's Salmon Poetry is one of the consoling realities of Irish cultural life. That it exists still is a joy, a beacon and a lesson in the power of permanent work.*'

THOMAS McCARTHY

Over forty years and six hundred volumes later Salmon Poetry is going strong. Poetry Ireland was party to the launch of many of these volumes and an enduring memory is of Jessie Lendennie and Siobhán Hutson descending on Poetry Ireland, in a whirlwind of energy and enthusiasm, for these launches, which took place—in those peripatetic days—in various venues around the city centre. This short article has been gathered from conversations with those who have been involved with both Salmon Poetry and Poetry Ireland over some of those forty years, I am honoured to have been asked to contribute.

The uniqueness of Salmon Poetry resides in its dream and its vision of creating greater access for both poets and the public to a broader range of voices, viewpoints and vistas, regardless of age, class, gender and nation, at a time when this was not common in Ireland. Former Chair of Poetry Ireland Mary Shine Thompson writes that 'In the dark days of the nineteen-eighties, Salmon Poetry was instrumental in steadying the poetry publishing business which was listing precariously eastwards and was manned predominantly by male poets... refuse[ing] to be bound exclusively by economic imperatives. Its optimism and risk-taking brought balance, nurturing alternative voices, offering unknown poets—many unfamiliar with the minefields of established Irish poetry politics—the gold of a published first collection.'

Part of the Poetry Landscape

'Salmon Poetry is a small Irish press with a strong and positive international reputation... and a significant, and important, force in poetry publishing—on both wings of the Atlantic!' says poet and publisher Seamus Cashman.

Salmon has always been part of that landscape for me, and for many others, including the Director of the Arts Council, Maureen Kennelly, who commented: 'Rita Ann Higgins's *Goddess on the Mervue Bus* was one of the first poetry books I bought and I still remember the potent charge that it gave to me. From this early success, Salmon Poetry has been responsible for bringing to light some of the finest writers of poetry. Their attention to women's voices has been especially notable and for that we all owe them an enduring debt.'

The idea of delivering a 'charge' is an apt way of thinking about Jessie Lendennie, the driving force behind Salmon Poetry. In varying manifestations, and over forty years, Salmon has succeeded in bringing a diverse range of voices to the attention of the public. As poet Nessa O'Mahony remarked, 'If Jessie Lendennie and Salmon didn't exist, countless poets who were encouraged to find their place in the publishing world because of her example simply wouldn't have persisted. She opened doors when others guarded them.'

Opening doors for both established voices and new voices, on both sides of the Atlantic, is the constant metaphor that emerges when talking to people about Salmon. One of those voices is Irish American poet, and friend, Richard Halperin who wrote that 'Jessie loved my poems, published me when no one was yet used to my voice, didn't give a rap what category I was in... and, as an editor, knew immediately what was in my best interest which I sometimes do not.' Richard points to her care for poets, a sentiment echoed by many to whom I spoke when preparing this piece.

Poet and editor of *The White Page/An Bhileog Bhán: 20th Century Irish Women Poets*, Joan McBreen, which began life as part of an MA in Womens' Studies with WERRC in UCD, back in the 1990s, where I first met Joan, and was subsequently published by Salmon in 1999, was also until recently a board member of Poetry Ireland. Joan remembers attending workshops with Jessie Lendennie in a room over Mick Taylor's on Dominick Street in Galway. She credits these workshops with her becoming a poet: 'When Jessie Lendennie finally managed to have me understand what it meant to find my voice, a door opened in my head.'

Poetry Ireland Review 92 (28-31: 2007) features an appreciation by Maurice Harmon. In this rich and honest appreciation of Salmon and Jessie Lendennie, Maurice cites her 'dedication... commitment, courage and vision... Without her many of us would not have made our way as poets.' It is fitting, therefore, to end with a poem by Joan McBreen, the poem in which she found her voice:

My Father

My father
was a lonely man
whose fifty years
at sea
had left
no deeper blue
in his eyes.

Once in spring
at Lissadell
he picked bluebells
for my mother
and his eyes
looked different.

He fought
death
a frightened man,
hauled
to unknown rocks
from an ocean
he could
not navigate.

I wonder nights now
what lonely bay
he sails in
and does he
quote his lines of Yeats
and smoke his pipe
and drink the whiskey
for the pain.

(From *The Wind Beyond the Wall* (Storyline Press)
and *Winter in the Eye: New & Selected Poems* (Salmon)

NESSA O'MAHONY

Visiting the publisher

Knockeven 2014

This is how I remember it.
The slow bends up from Doolin,
the sky widening, the sense of an edge
somewhere, a sweep of cliffs
when we went too far, missed the turning
for the boreen, the donkeyed field.
Then a low wall and a bungalow.

And suddenly it was all whirl,
pulse after pulse of collie energy,
nails scrabbling on the floor
as the pack raced from one side to the other.
You couldn't tell where one dog ended,
another began in tail and rump and hair,
tongues lolling in juggernaut joy
past chicanes of books and boxes
and back again for yet another circuit.

I'm sure there was much to talk about
—portents and poets and slim volumes—
but I don't remember that. I do recall
your smile, your contented shrug
as a leaf blew and the pack took off again.

MARY O'MALLEY

Cherry Tree Carol

I called the kings, expecting faded
colours, old cardboard men, jaded
from expectation and travel. Instead
they whirled in the air, turbanned
young, rings flashing ruby and gold.

In spite of what they know, they glowed
before me for a minute or an hour.
Centuries spooled out around them, lures
cast from a rod across the flat surface
of the trembling elements.

I called Mary, pregnant and homeless
in spite of what I know and how it ends.
She came to give birth again in a shed
warmed by the sharp stink of a wolf's breath
or the fug of cattle and ass.

It wasn't the birth I wanted but the story
of this strange child in the womb
that ordered a cherry tree to bow down
low to my mother's knee
to satisfy her gravid craving and ours.

In spite of the nails and the lumbering beast
the moon and the stars will sail under his feet,
the masked moon and her icy stars.

JAMES O'SULLIVAN

Market

Hounds rest at the foot of a van—
tarps rise, scattered about canals—

Cheese and wooden tulips, bike locks,
thousands, hang, while structures buckle—

He walks by the dull brass, dead clocks,
chessboards and fragmented sextants—

He brings the porcelain to his eye,
then places it back among the trinkets.

Seeking poise, he carries on—
hoping, someday, to fine something of his own.

ALICE PETTWAY

Solstice

Infusion of spruce tips and wild geranium
　　just-bloomed yarrow

the sun hidden all day
a falcon fishing
　　　between the clouds.

　　　　　We watched her
all of us together
our longest selves

stretching into the shallow arc
　　　　　of the shadows.

She never caught a fish.

And still we watched,
wanting
to bear witness

to the breaking

of beak through flesh,
the cracking open

　　of a new season.

STEPHEN ROGER POWERS

Galway Bay

for Jessie

The house I grew up in now has two storeys.
I haven't been inside in forty years.
One day I'll ask the owners for a look around.
I want to see where they put the stairs.
I walk around the house I live in now,
hope to discover a door I'd not noticed
that leads to a room we never knew.
The new room brightens like curtains opening.
We pull back the dust covers from the furniture,
gather them, shake them outside, hurry in
because we are enamored with the surprise.
Does a house feel? If so, I can't explain
how it must feel when unknown rooms are discovered.
Or when a storey is added.
What happens to attics in that case?
Are trunks and old photo albums moved elsewhere,
or do you build the story around them?
My favorite story to tell about this was in the Claddagh,
Upper Fairhill Road, Auburn House,
dark and empty under renovation
for a second-storey addition.
I was invited to look in the window,
where I imagined the place under a spell,
modest outside, spacious and airy as a manor
when you enter, perfect view of the bay upstairs
waiting for floral drapes to part.

LIZ QUIRKE

Vaya Con Dios

for Mikey

*"'Vaya con Dios,' she said. But Clare knew now, as she had not four years ago,
that this is what the Spaniards say."*

> —Kate O'Brien, *As Music and Splendour*

A Thursday between here and after, we venture towards a session
in Spanish Point. My father, your grandfather suspended ill,
isn't anywhere, isn't even dead, so in his name tonight,
I put miles between my car and Killimer's ferry dock,
grasp the invite to join the kind-eyed boys and you
and we chase cold pints and assembly along Clare's tattered coast.

This "second-summer", you've set your anchor to drag the river
where I send all my words to swim. At Ennistymon,
on the banks of the Inagh, we begin, my sister's second son and I,
to churn up such mischief as will bridge the decade I've waited
    for this company.
Composed, all six-foot-plus, at the back of Salmon's weekday theatre,
you wait, bear respectful witness to the friendships a poetic life can forge.

After, we thaw in Lahinch's Shamrock, grow warmer still out the
    back of The Nineteeth.
You translate what you know of your prodigal aunt into who you
    see in this bar.
And I understand I can't boast traction in the story from your hand,
know little beyond your babyhood and snippets doled out across
    the distance,
but as Duarte saw the soul-sure "split" in Kate O'Brien's Clare,
for years I've seen how heart-stark scrutiny can untether a body.

You tell me you have come of age alongside rivers,
Lee, Shannon, Los Besòs and onwards now to the Inagh,
and brave in this late hour, you ease towards memories of my own,
how I knew when I told how it all transpired who said what and when
I arm you with keepsakes from my travels, souvenirs of leaving and returning
show you, nephew, that our lives don't have to look so different from the rest

At The Armada, Willie Clancy is in his afters and a bouncer caught
    by a light-quick trick
sends me to dive, delighted, deep into the swell of my purse. I surface, haul
a squall-torn license, confront a likeness from my tough days of being
    asked and telling
and then all around us is carnival as the singers blast out The Rose
    of Tralee.
We reel and jig through talk of your grandfather, my father,
    make promises that we
will have more nights like this, safe from all that is approaching
    us in the dark.

ELIZABETH REAPY

Science Answers Now!

QUESTION:

The fabric of what we know of as space is compressed by gravity and other natural laws to create matter—solar systems, stars, planets, rocks, the ocean, plants, animals, us. We are all diverse physical designs of this cosmic material.

An atom is the fundamental unit of matter. Energy is a property that exists in an atom, either moving or having the potential to move. Quantum physics states space is what exists in a split atom. So is energy space? And what mysterious force decides the movement? Life?

Without the weight of political or cultural conditioning on a word, life can be an interchangeable term for god, creator—for love.

In essence, are we condensed expressions of love, interacting with other condensed expressions of love, surrounded by and inspired by love?

Are we like some sort of finely chopped onions, carrots, potatoes and plump tomatoes of love contained in a warm mug of love soup, made tenderly in the kitchen of love to serve at love's table, to love with love by love?

ANSWER:

Science Answers Now! is a website to assist primary school children with their homework projects. Please seek an appropriate forum for your questions.

THOMAS DILLON REDSHAW

The Shipwreck

after Claude-Joseph Vernet, 1772

A bolt of lightning such as Zeus threw
Points out a whitened city on a far shore,
One of the safe ports.
                The storm blows
The barque onto the rocky foreshore.
The aft mast divides the scene into two
Right triangles & points to a broken tree
On the cliff.
           Drenched, blown about,
Players costumed in blue, white, red
Strive for rescue, dare escape down halyards
Over perfect waves—hanging men
Wanting rescue.

The clowns haul away sea chests, tuns of wine.
A mother laments. A youth mourns his girl.
Only the skinny hound is silent. The gnomes
Of the cliff face cry out, growl down,
Sniff the stormy air.
             In the highest, clearest
Plash of storm surge, the Hag of the Shore
Coldly decants scorn that no plate or
Page in an encyclopedia can account for.

2009

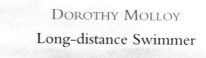

DOROTHY MOLLOY

Long-distance Swimmer

salmonpoetry

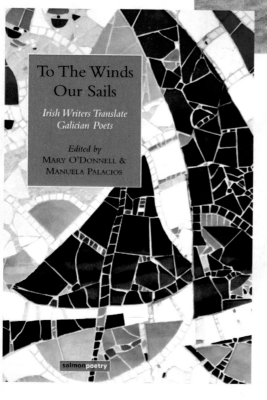

To The Winds
Our Sails

*Irish Writers Translate
Galician Poets*

Edited by
MARY O'DONNELL &
MANUELA PALACIOS

salmonpoetry

2010

MAD FOR MEAT

KEVIN SIMMONDS

salmon poetry

2011

2012

THANKS FOR NOTHING, HIPPIES

SARAH CLANCY

salmon poetry

BERTHA ROGERS

Poet on the Cliffs of Moher

*With gratitude to Jessie Lendennie,
Poet & Publisher, Salmon Poetry*

She walks the sea cliffs,
poems winding, following
on weighted sea breeze,
traveling with wide wings.

Words come to her
on blue wind, white clouds—
birds migrating, fog songs.

Earth-stone burrows here,
but new poems grow—
from her hands they bloom.

She names them flowers,
calls them butterflies—
birds blossoming,
petals turning like pages
in the boundless book of words.

She is the nest,
the refuge of runes—
poems come to her,
they flutter and perch,
they stop at her open hands,
pleased to be found.

CAROL RUMENS

Waterways

for Jessie Lendennie

Language is guiltless, even
if its first crossing-places
were excavated by swords.

You found trapped water, clear
and circling in the clutter
of false starts and their memory,

worked it free, a solid
innocence, shaping outwards
like an aquatic mammal

or a fish—a brilliant salmon—
or a poem—since poems, too,
swim in good solutions.

Language climbed out of its rust,
un-riven, un-armed, received
its voices, its listening.

LEX RUNCIMAN

The Opening Page

for Jessie & Siobhán and all the Salmon Family

The opening page says surprise,
and what is that light, that dark, that shape?
How does sound mean? And quiet—
what is that? And song or speech—
which came first with a cradled touch, a swaying?

I can hardly recall not reading—
that emptiness crowded now, crowded out
by too many nights in the eagerness of pages.
Then poems came, and reading them aloud
let me be any voice, composed, not myself,

yet in my ears it was my voice saying
"I will arise and go now," saying
"The bird was made of paper, red and blue,"
saying "A palsy of regrets.
No. I won't go back."

In a culture of the book,
no book without the author, yes,
but no books without the fierce and dogged
makers of books: and so to them this praise
and this thanks be—all bells rung loud, thanks be.

QUOTES:
William Butler Yeats, "The Lake Isle of Innisfree"
Jessie Lendennie, "Daughter"
Eavan Boland, "Mise Eire"

MICHAEL SCHMIDT

Back in 2002 when Carcanet was publishing Mary O'Malley's *The Boning Hall*, Mary gave gracious thanks to Jessie Lendennie of Salmon Press 'who published the collections from which the selections in this volume are taken'. By then the Press had come of age and moved from Galway to County Clare, and Jessie had built up her list which included Moya Cannon, Eva Bourke and other key women writers, Irish and international. As 'an alternative voice in Irish literature' it focussed on the west of Ireland and built up a distinctive list of women writers in particular. I take off my hat to Jessie, Salmon's founder, in this anniversary year: from her list Carcanet has learned a good deal about Irish poetry. Her concentration on new poets has given opportunities to many. Some of her risks may not have taken hold (that's the nature of editorial risk) but others have grown into defining presences. Like Carcanet, Salmon grew out of a magazine and out of a specific locale. One day I hope to visit its headquarters in Ennistymon, County Clare, shake the founder by the hand, and thank her in person. And visit The Salmon Bookshop and Literary Centre, a comprehensive achievement which is remarkable and, for a mere publisher, enviable: how wonderful to be able to offer readers and writers a bookshop and a performance and study space as well as a publishing house!

Michael Schmidt OBE FRSL
General Editor, *PN Review*
Publisher and Managing Director,
Carcanet Press Limited

JOHN W. SEXTON

The Sight of Everything

Muhammed Faris (b. 1951), Syrian astronaut.
Crewman aboard the Mir space station 1987.

Was he but ten when he saw the hooded bulbuls
in the fig tree, the garden loud with their noise?
They were bright and free between the lobed leaves,
flittering and present, there and then gone.
The garden was theirs to have, and so was the sky.
Was it in the deep Allepo nights of his childhood
that he first scratched his eyes on the stars?

Years later, from his round window in Mir,
he could see the whole world below him;
not a border beheld, not a sign that said country.
From there, Syria had no beginning or end,
but was part of everything he could look down on.

When he came back from his sojourn in space,
from those seven days twenty-three hours and five minutes,
a school, an airport, roads were named after him. He became
a larger part of Syria; but not of the Syria he'd seen from space,
that distant Syria that was beyond borders, beyond even a name.

He was installed at the air force college, a mentor
to fighter pilots. He had become a caged bulbul.

In August 2012, after twenty-five years in his air force
cage, he drove with his family over the border
and into Turkey. None of which he had ever seen
from above, for from there the world was just the world.

He abides in his exile, a refugee; grounded for now.
But he has seen the bulbuls take the garden as their own,
and his eyes have been scratched by the stars,
and he can see through the borders of men.

LORNA SHAUGHNESSY

Sky Lullaby

The skylark lifts its song so high
We forget how hard it is to die.

—Gabriela Mistral

A wreath of green birdsong around your bed,
robin, blackbird, finch and wren.

The lark will rise before the sun
to draw it up on the thread it has spun
from silken strands of sky and wind.

Shot like an arrow from the ground
it halts on high, a bodiless sound
that hangs in the air from quavers and trills.

There is no smoke in the skylark's house,
no fire to betray its whereabouts
just a cup of grass and hair underfoot.

So step carefully through the hours of day,
know the lark's eggs are easy prey
to the hungry rat and trampling boot.

Its only defence is its song to the sun,
the quaver in throat and quiver in lung
as the merlin wheels its taloned hunt.

Listen: darkness has its own strains,
the toot and trundle of distant trains
soft chime of keys in the stirring air.

A wreath of green birdsong around your bed,
robin, blackbird, finch and wren.

The lark will rise before the sun
to draw it up on the thread it has spun.
Sleep now, and wake to its song.

EILEEN SHEEHAN

Deciduous

There was a girl and the path through the woods
was the only path. It was winter and the scene was
clean and all verticals. Serious green to grey to softer grey and
lines of solid black, dexter and sinister. Future and past
unknowable. Trees sang the story of trees
their long shadows.
                          Her hands on the skin
of a tree. Scarred like her knee and warm
to her touch. Dark fissures for beetles
to nest in. Silver scribble of lichen displaying
a traceable lexicon. Acid and alkaline. Squidgy green moss
to the north side. Yellow lichens sang the story of air
its pure components.

                          Stood at the base of the tree and
grounded. Her feet where small creatures burrowed and
foraged. Debris of autumn rotting down
into earth. Leaf mould and carcass. Reduction happening
so quietly. And the floor sang the story of fungus
its insatiable hunger.

                          And the path from the woods was
the right path. Footstep and footstep. And the girl sang the story
of trees, the story of air. Sang the story of hunger. With the trees
at attention.

And the woods sang the song of a child.

KNUTE SKINNER

A Different Woman

You could say that Audrey and I first met
in the hotel's coffee shop.

But I had noticed her just the day before
as she cut in front of me
to claim the very best place
in the parking lot.

And again at the cigarette vending machine
as she bumped ahead and sent
my coins all over the floor.

In the coffee shop I found her a different woman.
At the cashier's counter she stood in front of me,
and—much to my surprise—
she suggested we share a table.

Well, we did share a table, and since then
I have learned to share a lot more.
Including the looks of annoyance
whenever she surges ahead
to lay claim to anything choice.

But we do share a bed now, and that
is enough to make it worthwhile
again and again and again.

JO SLADE

Maman

Birds without nests wander the roofs
of women only houses
tv's colour their feathers gold
when light reflects up
from rooms with children

Children are angels without a heaven
they used to be robins
we could speak with them
they were brave & curious
they laid eggs in in our palms
blue ovals like planets

When terror came
they hid in derelict churches
mothers wove masks from waste plastic
fledglings were born
mouths crusted with trichomoniasis

When storms raged & earth burned
they flew above the sludge
mothers stood in the singe
holding the world's detritus

Balanced above the trash
a spider who strayed from the world
was weaving invisibly
the unspeakable words—
east swept west into the ocean

ision is sudden & illuminative
an extreme childhood means
the shadow extinguishes—
the child is transparent
naked   but protected

It is night when I look up—
moons comfort me:
embryo planets that drift
in wombs of light
women & children raised
into the stratosphere—
incandescent orbs of love

NOTES:

The title *Maman* is a reference to the large spider
sculpture 'Maman' by Louise Bourgeois, 1999.

Trichomonasis is a disease of young birds, though
not particularly robins.

DAMIAN SMYTH

Sit Your Ground

Horace, Ode 1.11

You needn't bother your arse about tomorrow. It's no business of yours,
Leuconoë, how many days I have left, or you, so quit that—
Reading out the starsigns from the *Sun*. Take it on the chin, regardless.
Whether there are more winters ahead, or this is the last I'll see breaking
Bottles at Tyrella Beach, just pass the Mundies Warm South African Tawny
Over here. Life's short as it is, don't go watering it down with big hopes.
The more chit-chat there is, the days only go faster by. So, suck it up.
Trust nothing. Like you, the future's ugly enough to look after itself.

GERARD SMYTH

Two for Jessie

I *American Troubadour*

When the show was over the man who shouted *Judas*
disappeared, but what he said was written
into the annals. The troubadour went on,
covering his tracks so that no one could catch him
by collar or cuff. No pause for rest,
harmonica hanging from his neck.
One hand on the Bible, the other deciding
between Shakespeare, Homer, *Leaves of Grass*.
Southbound. Northbound. Bound to his purpose:
the climb to Parnassus,
harder to reach than Louisiana, Tulsa, Kansas.
Sometimes he calls himself Jack Frost,
gets caught in the spin of words from his loom,
saying under his breath *Be honest with me,
I'll be honest with you.*
Close up the half-smile shows its cracks.
On stage it sometimes falls from his mask.

II *Kerouac*

Kerouac said he saw his visions in newsreel grey:
his scenes from boyhood, a lost brother
who stayed in his dreams,
his own shadow running at speed on a football field
where he became a hero in the League.
Nothing could stop his dance to the rhythms,
the beats of typewriter jazz.
Kerouac said that leaving a childhood house
was *a catastrophe of the heart*...
And he knew about that, so many addresses
between Moody Street and Ozone Park.
He worshipped Thomas Wolfe and Lester Young,
the bebop he heard in Harlem clubs.
Like an outlaw on the run he took the open road,
followed the long white line
to his heaven of the mind:
Mexican sunlight, a bottle of Skid Row wine.

A. E. STRINGER

A Salmon-Falcon for Jessie

From sea depths upward and sky-high down, it rides
the earth's unearthliest currents, fins and wings

interwoven as wind into surf into coastline.
It is *Sky and Water I*, Escher's great woodcut,

a diamond checkered in black and white, set
inside a square. The picture's midline ripples through

a vague tessellation. Then ten birds ascend, evolve
into clarity through ten fish in descent. At the nadir

a gray fish glides, elegantly scaled, and at the apex,
a feathery black waterfowl in flight. The diamond

of their genesis is framed by the artist's own etched
horizontals. The depths of the print are darkness

itself and the sky milk-white, backgrounds in polarity
to the creatures' twin emergences. What's this

inshore, out of frame? A woman walking a dog,

making photographs, making books, caught in the act
of perpetual interplay. It's a rough beast: salmon-

falcon, woman-dog, trading shapes off the coast
of Doolin as an afternoon of surf and sunlight

strikes the rocks of age, their enduring forms
partaking of light and dark in equal parts, in flux.

As the hour comes round again, she notes how all
springs from one thing at a time. The salmon's skill

is taking flight against the downrush of thaw, ever
upriver toward rebirth. Here is a vignette of every

inter-genesis the mind, a–ramble, may dwell upon:
word and image, ink and paper, poem and voice.

Light and dark and feather and scale. Stillness.
Movement. Pattern, dimension. *Sub specie aeternitatis*.

2013

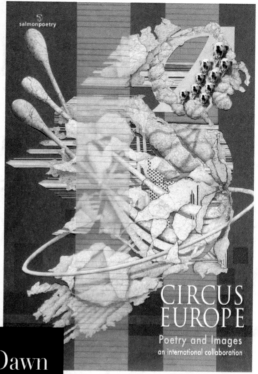

2014

2015

2016

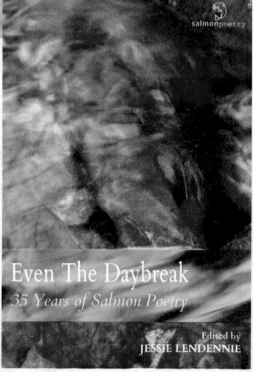

ANNE TANNAM

Boundless

'O, reason not the need. Our basest beggars
Are in the poorest thing superfluous.'

—King Lear

They discovered me buried between two humans;
the place where we lay guarded by basalt blocks
—sprayed red with hematite—
to keep out scavengers, hungry to strip
our carbon-dated bones white clean.

O, the speculation when we were discovered—
perplexed faces hovering above us,
scientific minds grappling with what they'd found.

Was I the first of my kind: *Canis Lupis Familaris,*
my wild lupine ancestors roaming the earth
a thousand score years before?

What purpose did I serve those that lay beside me—
I, who died so young of canine distemper,
unable to hunt, to scavenge; what good was I
to him, to her, to them?

O, foolish questions, foolish minds.

> Have you never sat close to a fire, watched sparks rise
> into the blue-black, star-blessed sky; the rustling forest
> briefly silenced; your hand stroking the soft belly
> of the sleeping animal by your side?

CAROLYN L. TIPTON

Birdbath

The birds haven't found it yet.
I worry about them, flying through air
thick with smoke from fires counties away.
I thought maybe they'd want to wash their wings,
so I cleaned out the old birdbath, filled it
with fresh water, floated a flower
as an offering.

But I think I am the one who needs the cleansing.
Not just from smoke, but from anger, and
from feeling like a stone, small center of
concentric circles of sorrow: the outermost,
the planet's tragedy; then, our country's chaos;
California's conflagrations; and at the heart of it,
the inadequate translation of presence, of touching,
into merely talking to a screen.

I hope they find it soon. I want to see them
no longer heavy with soot, but light enough
to lift their wings into full spread, released
from accumulated grime, able to rise up, renewed,
into a sky that wishing has, for once,
turned back to blue.

DANIEL TOBIN

At Chronain's Well

Carran, Co. Clare

Coins in the stone basin
more in passage than in blessing
where the sourceless
pools from its ground below.

Still they hang cloth strips here
on the hawthorn, the frayed
rainbow weathering
to a blanched
and frittering remnant.

Above, in the walled field,
the saint also waits
beneath his rock tabernacle
beside the un-roofed church
with its figures staring
rain-worn past the hazels
to the sea.

Walk seven times clockwise
around this tufted mound,
tilth-poor, the beads
shackled lovingly
between wrist and knuckle,

keeping mindful of the cross,
the cracked, armless, tilting
stump of it
that cannot be mended ever—

seen whole
now only in the soul's life
beyond all manifest and
measure.

PETER VAN DE KAMP

Zach

Hark that bark!
That latrant grief
Is blatant love.
It was a dog's life—
The top dog
That left you home,
His hair everywhere,
His dog days done,
And no more bones to pick,
But not alone:
He's gone to all the dogs
For whom you shed a tear,
To be what he just meant
For you, for you, for good.

DRUCILLA WALL

Lullaby for Grandson Gavin, on His Seventh Week

Smoke from the fires in California has reached us on the Mississippi shore. Hazed sun since morning. White ash dressing the garden. It would be four days driving to live embers raining and distant screams of deer and rabbits burning in the blackening hills.

Big sister Sweetie Pie is three years old, wears every necklace from Grandma's basket, has a dance party in Granddad's study. Jingle jangle. And nap time is lap time with my little boy blue, already in the six-month size pajamas.

Rocka baby and read my phone. Ads just for me dangle earrings that shine like the northern lights, then the amazing eco-jet personal butt cleaner.

Rocka rocka, baby, rocka rocka roo

Mice sing to each other. We cannot hear them. In the wild grasses and leaf litter they lilt, ending always in an upward note. Ultrasonic, recordable.

Ah rocka rocka, baby, ah rocka rocka roo

Trees send aid through the fungi of their roots. Mother nourishment vibrates upward in saplings drawn in the network we cannot see. Crowns tower in the canopy just shy of each other. The root embrace is enough.

Ah rocka rocka, baby, ah rocka rocka roo

Fish become dogs if you feed them at the boat slip. Their eyes open, mouths flipping up to your hand. Pet them on the head. Gently gently, the current swift at the center.

Ah rocka rocka, baby, ah rocka rocka roo

Wind cuts from the west across the caged tomato vines. I shield your sister's slender form cupped in my bending body. We are picking all the green ones before the killing frost. Leave the smallest for the squirrels, the rabbits and mice. Littles for little mouths, she says.

And rocka rocka, baby, rocka rocka roo

Filaments twist across the universe holding galaxies unknown to us. Lullaby. Night is rolling ash wind over cold clay. I will keep you hidden from virus, flame, and poison. You will bury me someday.

EAMONN WALL

Dear Charlotte: A Visit to the City

Items gathered from Haworth Parsonage
and London's National Portrait Gallery
are on exhibit today at the Morgan Library.
Miraculously on Madison Avenue
many sundry treasures are housed as one
again, the Brontë materials path-worn
to this temporary New York home.
1847 when the great trio by three sisters,
first editions under glass today, saw light.

There are two violinists playing classical
in the atrium café of the Morgan Library:
I wish they could be stopped so I might
read uninterrupted Rachel Cusk's *Outline*,
this year's must-read book. Fortunately
today, no TVs evident so some pause
from the endless byline. Looking up, then
into the emptiness grazing, I see one joyful
Caribbean mother, her child having fallen
into sleep, catching that faint breath song
of the miracle she has guided into life.

Immigrants: we start each day over cereal
and coffee, boarding buses, chasing
parking spaces closest to the office
door, worrying over shoes & hair, hoping
to gather again at evening time, sparrows
taking flight above our roofs. I have been
by Mrs Gaskell's *Life of Charlotte Brontë*,
and your family's many poems and fictions
over many decades wandering mesmerized.
We have, all of us, come hither from elsewhere.

GORDON WALMSLEY

Evening Light

Starlings in the trees
waiting in rows
before the final lifting

There is an almost silence
before they blend into the needles
hiding or silhouetting.

We climb the dune to the west
watching the sun bleed into the evening,
the red flow vanishing,
as they lift into thousands

Stream across the sands
finding, at last, a nocturnal home
in the grasses by the sea.

They leave me with a question,
a mystery more ripe
than any conundrum.

SANDRA ANN WINTERS

Pandemic

I will not see you Ireland.
I will not walk the
western coastline, hugged
with islands and peninsulas.
I will not stroll across
the ancient, corrugated lazybeds
of Inishbofin and Kilcrohane.
I will miss stroking
the stone circle of Kenmare,
and squeezing into the dark
passageway of Newgrange.
I will miss the pubs with
Michael, Siobhan, Sean,
pints of Guinness,
plates of mussels.
As I walk across the Burren,
I will not photograph the golden gorse,
the common spotted orchid,
the tufted vetch,
the Dingle fishermen
unloading their catch.
I will miss the rain.

JOSEPH WOODS

Most Appealing Eyes

Adorable Leamington, our inherited black lab and named after the royal
spa town for whatever reason by your first set of owners,
and which we quickly abbreviated to 'Lemmy'. Reluctant guard dog
but eminent family pet and legendary sleeper on lawns, your black coat
assiduously sucked up the sun and just occasionally, having had enough,

you'd throw yourself with a heavy flump in the shade of the verandah.
Or join with Angel, your sprightlier golden-retriever companion
in the search for phantom bones; diggers and destroyers of garden beds.
And while neither dog ever fetched anything, in twilight, their nutty half-hour
was made up of pretend scraps and fights our cats superciliously stared upon.

Originally 'rescue dogs', we were your third set of owners, but had you
the longest, five years, an eternity for our daughter who once insisted
despite your greying jowls in entering you for the local dog competition,
a prospect more Home Counties than Shona in Harare. Lemmy, nonplussed,
sauntered off with a rosette for 'Most Appealing Eyes', a category that was new

to us, and with enough treats to last an age; a tartan dog-blanket quickly
shredded and tubs of biscuits, gravy and even doggy *boerewors*.
When Covid came, our pets in care, we left for home for four months
and while summer appeared in Ireland, winter was harsh in Harare. All survive
and on return, greetings were effusive with Lemmy, unsteady but tail-wagging

The following week with friends over, we sat on the verandah while the girls
played on swings and Lemmy lay close by, content perhaps that laughter
had returned to the dark evenings. Next morning, shortly after sunrise,
he lay stretched out and asleep forever on the lawn. We placed him within
our walls and under the flame tree and the leaves he liked to rustle in.

SANDRA YANNONE

The Garden

for Jessie

Before the day takes off, before
I watch the crow lift into the morning sky
as if from out of the painting above

her fireplace mantle, I step
into her garden waiting and breathe
dear life into my wanderlusted lungs.

One wall of the garden, a wild
tangle, the other an ocean of ivy.
A single pink tulip skies

toward the day from the ground
below, reminds me that the year is still
early, to say nothing of this morning,

to say plenty that I'll leave
unsaid about last night's spells
cast into the fire. At one end

of the garden, an arched stone passage
that leads to the building listing
with books. At the other end, a studio

unfinished, a sanctuary city all by itself.
Between both, a door that opens
to a ruin of stacked doors, each door

waiting to bestow entry
to somewhere other
than the garden

which needs no doors, when
so lovely this singular April morning,
the garden dares

in its absence of the obvious
to suggest every one of her
beloved anticipated stems.

2017

salmonpoetry

Migrant
Shores

With calligraphies by
Hachemi Mokrane

Irish, Moroccan & Galician Poetry
Edited by Manuela Palacios

2018

Songs from the Blue River
PAUL KINGSNORTH

One
Small
Sun
Paulann
Petersen

2019

2020

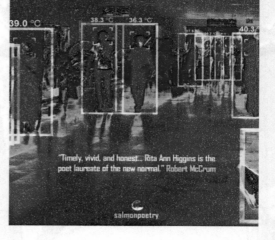

Rita Ann Higgins
Pathogens Love A Patsy

Pandemic & Other Poems

39.0 °C   38.3 °C   36.3 °C   40.3

"Timely, vivid, and honest... Rita Ann Higgins is the
poet laureate of the new normal." Robert McCrum

salmonpoetry

Contributor Biographical Notes

MICHAEL ALLEN works for homeless charity Focus Ireland, where he is responsible for the organisation's advocacy, research and communication work. He previously spent eight years as the General Secretary of the Irish Labour Party. Prior to that, he was the General Secretary of the Irish National Organisation of the Unemployed (INOU). He is a co-founder of Salmon Publishing.

MARCK L. BEGGS is the author of four collections of poetry—*Godworm*, *Libido Café*, *Catastrophic Chords*, and *Blind Verse*—the three most recent of which were published by Salmon Poetry. He lives in Little Rock, Arkansas where he also performs with his folk-rock band, dog gods. In 2009, he was selected as one of the top 10 sexiest vegetarians by PETA. www.marckbeggs.com

Born in 1959, DERMOT BOLGER is a novelist, playwright and poet. His fifteenth work of fiction, *Secrets Never Told*, appeared in 2020. As editor of Raven Arts Press from 1977 to 1992, he has been proud to have known Jessie as a colleague since the early days of Salmon.

EVA BOURKE's most recent and seventh collection is *Seeing Yellow* (Dedalus Press, 2017). She co-edited with Vincent Woods *Fermata. Writings Inspired by Music* (Artisan House, 2016) and was awarded the Michael Hartnett Prize 2020 for *Seeing Yellow*. She is a member of Aosdána.

HEATHER BRETT is editor/founder of *Windows Publications* for 23 years. She has edited over 30 poetry & art anthologies including 10 Windows Publications Author & Artists Introductions Series. Her poem 'Testament' was commissioned by Cavan County Council and set to music by award winning composer Sean Doherty from Derry. Heather Brett has been Writer-in-Residence for counties Cavan, Louth, Longford and the Midlands Collaboration of Laois, Westmeath & Offaly.

BARBARA BROWN is Emeritus Professor of English Literature at Marshall University, Huntington, West Virginia. Since her retirement, she has resided in Dublin, where she works as an editor.

SIOBHÁN CAMPBELL acknowledges Jessie Lendennie's breadth of influence in reading and publishing, especially of the poetic diaspora, which enriches us all. Siobhan's fourth collection is *Heat Signature*—'a poet invested in words as powerful social currency.' (Compass). This follows *Cross-Talk* (Seren) and the Templar award-winning *That Water Speaks in Tongues*.

MOYA CANNON is an Irish poet with six published collections, the most recent being *Donegal Tarantella* (Carcanet). Music, particularly traditional Irish music, has always been a deep interest and is a constant theme. She has received the Brendan Behan Award and the O'Shaughnessy Award and was 2011 Heimbold Professor of Irish Studies at Villanova University. She was born in Co. Donegal and now lives in Dublin.

HÉLÈNE CARDONA's books include *Life in Suspension, Dreaming My Animal Selves* and the translations *Birnam Wood* by José Manuel Cardona (Salmon Poetry), *Beyond Elsewhere* (Gabriel Arnou-Laujeac, White Pine Press), *Ce que nous portons* (Dorianne Laux, Éditions du Cygne), *Walt Whitman's Civil War Writings* (WhitmanWeb). Her work has been translated into sixteen languages.

ALVY CARRAGHER is an Irish poet and author, based in Toronto. Her debut collection of poetry was published by Salmon Poetry, and her second poetry collection *The men I keep under my bed* is forthcoming. You can find out more about her work at www.alvycarragher.com

A journalist, magazine editor, legal author and media communications director for thirty years, ANNE CASEY is an award-winning Irish poet/writer and Australian government scholarship PhD researcher living in Australia. Author of two collections published by Salmon Poetry, with a third book forthcoming in 2021, her work is widely published internationally.

PAUL CASEY's second collection *Virtual Tides* was published by Salmon Poetry in 2016. It followed *home more or less* (Salmon, 2012) and *It's Not All Bad* (Heaventree, 2009). He teaches creative writing, edits the *Unfinished Book of Poetry* and promotes poetry in his role as director of Ó Bhéal, Cork.

SEAMUS CASHMAN founded Wolfhound Press in 1974. Now a workshop facilitator with adults and young people, he co-produced the children's film, *Stitched*. He has four books of poetry, two with Salmon, including *The Sistine Gaze* (2015), and edited two key young reader anthologies. He has given readings in Europe, America, Africa and the Middle East.

PATRICK CHAPMAN is a poet, fictionist and scriptwriter. He has published thirteen books since 1991, most recently *Open Season on the Moon* (Salmon, 2019) and *David Cronenberg* (non-fiction, Sonicbond, UK, 2020). He is a founder and co-editor of poetry magazine *The Pickled Body*.

SARAH CLANCY is a page and performance poet from Galway, she has three collections to her name, *Stacey and the Mechanical Bull* (Lapwing Press, Belfast, 2011) and *Thanks for Nothing, Hippies* (Salmon Poetry, 2012) and *The Truth and*

Other Stories (Salmon Poetry 2014). Along with fellow Galway poet Elaine Feeney she released a poetry CD called *Cinderella Backwards* in 2013. She has been placed or shortlisted in several of Ireland's most prestigious written poetry competitions including The Ballymaloe International Poetry Prize, The Patrick Kavanagh Award and The Listowel Collection of Poetry Competition.

GILLIAN CLARKE was National Poet of Wales from 2008 to 2016. She was awarded the Queen's Gold Medal for Poetry in 2010. Her *Selected Poems* was published by Picador in 2016, and her most recent collection, *Zoology*, appeared from Carcanet in 2017. Her version of the 7th century Welsh poem, *Y Gododdin*, appears from Faber in 2021.

JANE CLARKE is the author of two poetry collections, *The River* and *When the Tree Falls* (Bloodaxe Books 2015 & 2019), as well as an illustrated chapbook, *All the Way Home* (Smith|Doorstop 2019). Jane lives in Glenmalure, Co. Wicklow and combines poetry with creative writing teaching and mentoring. www.janeclarkepoetry.ie

RACHEL COVENTRY's poems have appeared in *The North, The Moth, Poetry Ireland Review, The Irish Times, The Shop*, and have featured on RTE Lyric FM. She holds a doctorate in philosophical poetics from NUIG. Her debut collection *Afternoon Drinking in the Jolly Butchers* (2018) is published by Salmon Poetry.

MAJELLA CULLINANE is an Irish writer based in New Zealand. Winner of the Sean Dunne Poetry Award, the Hennessy Award for Emerging Poetry and the Caselberg International Poetry Prize, she has published two poetry collections *Guarding the Flame*, Salmon Poetry, 2011 and *Whisper of a Crow's Wing*, Salmon Poetry and Otago University Press, 2018.

County Carlow native ELEANOR CUMMINS has a background in theatre and education. Her plays include *The Sacred Sow*, staged at the Prague Theatre Festival with the Prague Playhouse & in New York, and a 2016 commemorative play about her grand-aunt, nurse Margaret Kehoe, who was shot dead in 1916. Eleanor has also appeared as an actress in several short films, including *Men & Women*. Her poems have appeared in various journals and have often been inspired by her travels around the world teaching English and theatre. Eleanor currently lives in Ennistymon, County Clare, where she manages The Salmon Bookshop & Literary Centre.

Belfast-born poet GERALD DAWE moved to Galway in 1974 where he lived for many years. He has published over twenty books of poetry and non-fiction including *The Last Peacock* (2019) and *Looking Through You: Northern Chronicles* (2020). He is Fellow Emeritus, Trinity College, Dublin.

MARY DORCEY is a critically acclaimed fiction writer and poet. Her work is taught and researched in universities from North America to Europe, China and Africa. She was elected to the Aosdána, Ireland's academy of writers and artists, in 2010. She has published nine books, three of fiction and six of poetry. Her New and Selected Poems *To Air the Soul, Throw all the Windows Wide* was published by Salmon in 2017. She was the first woman in Irish history to campaign publicly for LGBT rights and the first to address the subject openly in literature. A lifelong feminist and gay rights activist, she was a founder member of Irishwomen United in 1975 and Women for Radical Change 1973. She is a Research Associate at Trinity College, Dublin where she has led seminars on women's literature and creative writing workshops for many years.

THEO DORGAN is a poet, and also a translator, novelist, non-fiction author, editor, and screenwriter for documentaries. His first two collections were published by Salmon, for which he has always been grateful. He is a member of Aosdána.

DAME CAROL ANN DUFFY is a British poet and playwright. She is a professor of contemporary poetry at Manchester Metropolitan University, and was appointed Poet Laureate in May 2009, resigning in 2019. Duffy's poetry collections included *Standing Female Nude* (1985), *The Other Country* (1990), *The World's Wife* (1999), and *Rapture* (2005). During this time she also authored such plays as *Take My Husband* (1982) and *Little Women, Big Boys* (1986). At the beginning of the 21st century, much of her work was written for children, including the picture books *Underwater Farmyard* (2002), *The Tear Thief* (2007), *The Princess's Blankets* (2009), and Dorothy Wordsworth's *Christmas Birthday* (2014), as well as the poetry collection *The Hat* (2007). She continued to produce verse for adults as well, notably issuing the collections *Love Poems* (2010), *The Bees* (2011), and *Sincerity* (2018). In 1996, Salmon Poetry published *The Salmon Carol Ann Duffy: Poems Selected and New 1985-1999.*

SUSAN MILLAR DUMARS has published five collections with Salmon. The most recent, *Naked: New and Selected Poems*, was launched in 2019. In 2020, Susan received an Irish Arts Council bursary allowing her to complete work on her second short story collection, *Cameos*. Susan and her husband Kevin Higgins have run the Over the Edge readings series in Galway since 2003.

MARTINA EVANS is an Irish poet, novelist and teacher. She is the author of eleven books of prose and poetry. Her first novel, *Midnight Feast*, won a Betty Trask Award in 1995 and her third novel, *No Drinking No Dancing No Doctors* (Bloomsbury, 2000), won an Arts Council England Award in 1999. *Burnfort, Las Vegas* (Anvil Press 2014) was shortlisted for the Irish Times Poetry Now Award 2015. *Mountainy Men*, a new narrative poem, was the recipient of a Grants for the

Arts Award in 2015 and *Watch*, a pamphlet, published by Rack Press in January 2016 was a Poetry Society Book Choice. *The Windows of Graceland, New & Selected Poems* was published by Carcanet in May 2016. Her latest collection *Now We Can Talk Openly About Men* was published by Carcanet in 2018.

ELAINE FEENEY is an Irish poet, novelist, and playwright. Her writing focuses on "the central themes of history, national identity, and state institutions, and she examines how these forces structure the everyday lives of Irish women." A former slam poetry winner, she has been described as "an experienced writer who has been wrestling with poetry on page and on stage since 2006" and in 2015 was heralded as "one of the most provocative poets to come out of Ireland in the last decade." Her work has been widely translated, including into Italian, Lithuanian, and Slovene. Salmon has published all three of her poetry collections, with the most recent, *Rise*, appearing in 2017.

VIVIANA FIORENTINO lives in Belfast. An award-winning poet in Italy, her poems appear in the anthology *Writing Home* (Dedalus Press). In 2019 she published a new poetry collection and a novel in Italy. Her poems, short stories and translations have appeared in international literature magazines (*as Nazione Indiana, FourXFour NI, Poethead, The Blue Nib, Paris Lit Up, Mantis*). She has co-founded two activist poetry initiatives: *Sky, You Are Too Big* and *Letters With Wings*. She is on the editorial staff of *Le Ortique*, (forgotten women artists' blog).

ANNE FITZGERALD's poetry collections are *Vacant Possession* (2017), *Beyond the Sea* (2012), *The Map of Everything* (2006) and *Swimming Lessons* (2001). She is a recipient of the Ireland Fund of Monaco Literary bursary at the Princess Grace Irish Library in Monaco. Anne teaches Creative Writing in Ireland and North America and lives in Dún Laoghaire, Co. Dublin. For further information see www.fortyfoot.press

JOHN FITZGERALD's collections include *Favorite Bedtime Stories* (Salmon Poetry) and *The Mind* (Salmon Poetry). Other works include *Talking to Rilke, Joe Smith,* and *Primate*. Publications include *World Literature Today, The Warwick Review, Taos Journal of Poetry and Art, December, From the Fishouse, The American Journal of Poetry, Plume,* and *Human and Inhuman Monstrous Poems.*

GABRIEL FITZMAURICE is the author of more than sixty books, including collections of poetry in English and Irish as well as several collections of verse for children and translations from the Irish. He has been described as "the best contemporary, traditional, popular poet in English" in *Booklist* (U.S).

JANICE FITZPATRICK SIMMONS took an MA from the University of New Hampshire. Her five collections of poetry have been reviewed in the USA, Ireland

and Great Britain. Widely published in literary journals in Ireland, England and America, Janice's work has appeared in major anthologies such as *A Rage for Order, The Backyards of Heaven, The Blackbird's Nest, Salmon: A Journey in Poetry 1981-2007* and *Irish American Poets since 1800.* After a period as assistant director of the Frost Place in New Hampshire, Janice founded the Poets' House in Portmuck in 1990, moved it to Falcarragh in 1996 and relocated its teaching function to Waterford in September 2005.

PHILIP FRIED is deeply grateful to Jessie Lendennie of Salmon Poetry, Ireland, for publishing six of his eight books of poetry, including his two most recent titles: *Squaring the Circle* (2017) and *Among the Gliesians* (2020). *The Guardian* has twice chosen his work for its "Poem of the Week" feature.

ANNE-MARIE FYFE has published five poetry collections & a literary/travel/personal poetry-&-prose memoir, *No Far Shore: Charting Unknown Waters* (Seren Books, 2019). Born in Cushendall, Co. Antrim, Anne-Marie lives in London where she works as a writer, arts organiser & freelance creative-writing teacher. She has run Coffee-House Poetry's readings & classes at London's leading live literature venue, the Troubadour, since 1997, is a Poetry Coordinator for the John Hewitt International Summer School, & is a former chair of the UK's Poetry Society. www.annemariefyfe.com

TESS GALLAGHER is the author of eleven books of poetry, including *Midnight Lantern: New and Selected Poems, Dear Ghosts,* and *Moon Crossing Bridge. Is, Is Not* was published by Bloodaxe Books in 2019. Gallagher spends time in Co. Sligo, Ireland, and also in her hometown of Port Angeles, Washington.

DAVID GARDINER studied at the University of Chicago, St. Thomas, UC Galway, Penn State, and Loyola University, Chicago where he studied under Seán Lucy, Robert Welch and Thomas Dillon Redshaw. He was founding editor of the journal, *An Sionnach* (2005–2010), Burns Scholar (Boston College), and Director of Irish Studies at Creighton University. Dr. Gardiner is currently director of Irish Studies at the University of St. Thomas and editor of the *New Hibernia Review.* He has authored over 60 journal publications and five books, including the Salmon poetry collections *Downstate* (2009) and *The Chivalry of Crime* (2015) as well as his forthcoming Salmon publication *Skenographia.*

PAUL GENEGA's long association with Salmon began in the 1980s with its eponymous lit mag. He has gone on to publish four collections with Salmon, most recently *Scullling on the Lethe* in 2018. Professor Emeritus at Bloomfield College, NJ, Paul lives with his husband Jim and Welsh springer Chance at the edge of the Hudson in Stuyvesant, NY.

DANI GILL is a writer and literary curator based in the west of Ireland. She is the current Artistic Director of Ennis Book Club Festival and National Literary Audience Development Officer for Words Ireland. Her debut poetry collection *After Love* was published by Salmon (2017). Her second collection will be released in 2021.

RICHARD W. HALPERIN was born in Chicago, holds Irish-U.S. dual-nationality and lives in Paris. His fourth Salmon collection is *Catch Me While You Have the Light*. His twelfth shorter collection for Lapwing Publications, Belfast, is *Under the Olive Tree*. His work is part of the UCD Irish Poetry Reading Archive.

Where Now Begins, Bloodaxe Books, is KERRY HARDIE's eighth collection. Her seventh, *The Zebra Stood in The Night*, was shortlisted for the Irish Times Award and she has won many prizes. She has also written two novels, a radio play (RTE), and is completing another novel. Her work has been widely translated and anthologised.

MAURICE HARMON, a scholar of Irish literature and an English-language poet, is Professor Emeritus of Anglo-Irish Literature and Drama at University College, Dublin, where he co-founded and formerly directed the Masters program in Irish Studies. Over the course of his career, Harmon was awarded numerous fellowships in the United States, teaching at Notre Dame University, Harvard University, and the Catholic University of America. In addition, Harmon was a long-time editor of several important journals in the field of Irish Studies, including *Irish University Review: A Journal of Irish Studies* (1970-1986) and *Poetry Ireland Review*.

ALAN HAYES is an editor, writer and equality activist, and publisher of Arlen House, Ireland's oldest and largest feminist publishing house. Among his publications are *Reading the Future: New Writing from Ireland* (Hodges Figgis, 2018), *Washing Windows: Irish Women Write Poetry* (Arlen House, 2017), *Irish Women's History* (Irish Academic Press, 2004), and *The Irish Women's History Reader* (Routledge, 2001).

MICHAEL HEFFERNAN is a retired professor of the Creative Writing program at the University of Arkansas. He lives in Fayetteville, Arkansas with his muse, Ann. He has enjoyed visiting Ireland and collaborating with Jessie on the five books of poetry he has so far had published with Salmon Poetry.

RACHAEL HEGARTY was born seventh child of a seventh child in Dublin and reared on the Northside of the city. She was educated by the Holy Faith Sisters in Finglas, the U. Mass. Bostonians in America, the M.Phil in Creative Writing at Trinity College, Dublin, and by the Ph.D. magicians at Queen's, Belfast.

Rachael lived, studied and worked in Boston and Japan for ten years. She now lives, back on the Northside, with her feminist husband and two beloved-bedlam boys. She is widely published in national and international journals and broadcast on RTÉ Radio 1. Rachael was the winner of the Francis Ledwidge Prize and Over the Edge New Writer of the year. Her debut collection, *Flight Paths Over Finglas* (Salmon Poetry), won the 2018 Shine Strong Award.

KEVIN HIGGINS has been described by *The Stinging Fly* magazine as "likely the most read living poet in Ireland." His sixth full collection of poems *Ecstatic* is forthcoming from Salmon.

RITA ANN HIGGINS was born in 1955 in Galway, Ireland. She divides her time between Galway and Spiddal. Her first five collections were published by Salmon Publishing. In 2018, Salmon published *Our Killer City*, a book of essays and poems. She was Galway County's Writer-in-Residence in 1987, Writer-in-Residence at the National University of Ireland, Galway, in 1994-95, Writer-in-Residence for Offaly County Council in 1998-99. She was Green Honors Professor at Texas Christian University in October 2000. Other awards include a Peadar O'Donnell Award in 1989, several Arts Council bursaries, and her collection "Sunny Side Plucked" was a Poetry Book Society Recommendation. She was made an honorary fellow at Hong Kong Baptist University in November 2006. Her most recent work, *Pathogens Love a Patsy: Pandemic and Other Poems* was published by Salmon in 2020.

ELEANOR HOOKER's third poetry collection and two chapbooks are due for publication in 2021. Her poetry and prose has been published internationally. Eleanor holds an MPhil (Distinction) in Creative Writing from Trinity College, Dublin. She's a Fellow of the Linnean Society of London, a helm and Press Officer for Lough Derg RNLI. www.eleanorhooker.com

RON HOUCHIN has 11 books, five from Salmon. His work has appeared in dozens of journals on both sides of the Atlantic. His love of Ireland and the Irish are what keep him going.

TIM JEANOTTE is husband of Siobhán, father of Eve, and son of Jessie. He is a board member of Salmon Poetry. He teaches French at a secondary school in Ennistymon, Co. Clare. He hopes to devote more of his time to writing.

FRED JOHNSTON's poems have appeared, most recently, in *The Spectator, The New Statesman*, and a short story in *Stand* magazine. In 1972, he received a Hennessy Literary Award for prose. In the mid-Seventies, with Neil Jordan and Peter Sheridan, he co-founded The Irish Writers' Co-operative (Co-Op Books.)

In 2002, he was a co-recipient of the Prix de l'Ambassade, Ireland. His most recent collection of short stories, *Dancing In The Asylum*, was published by Parthian. Fred has published nine collections of poems, four novels and two collections of short stories, one of which has been translated into French. His most recent collection of poetry, *Rogue States*, was published by Salmon in 2018.

JEAN KAVANAGH is an Irish poet living in Norway. She studied Irish Folklore and English Literature in UCD, Dublin, and has a Masters' Degree in Indigenous Studies from the Arctic University of Tromsø, Norway. Her work has been published in journals, showcase anthologies for the Galway Arts Centre, and in *Dogs Singing: A Tribute Anthology* (Salmon, 2011), and *Even the Daybreak: 35 Years of Salmon Poetry* (Salmon, 2016). In 2012 she was shortlisted for the Patrick Kavanagh Poetry Award. *Other Places*, her debut collection, was published in 2014, and was shortlisted for the Strong/Shine Award for Best First Collection in 2015. Her second collection, *How the Weather Was*, was published by Salmon in 2019.

COLM KEEGAN is a writer and poet from Dublin, Ireland. He has been shortlisted four times for the Hennessy New Irish Writing Award, for both poetry and fiction and won the All Ireland Poetry Slam in 2010. His first book *Don't Go There* was released to critical acclaim. His latest collection *Randomer* was published in 2014, also by Salmon Poetry.

DES KENNY is a bookseller at one of Ireland's most successful and long-lived bookshops, Kennys of Galway, and a long-time supporter of Salmon Poetry.

BRIAN KIRK's first poetry collection *After The Fall* was published by Salmon Poetry in 2017. His poem "Birthday" won Irish Poem of the Year at the An Post Irish Book Awards 2018. His short fiction chapbook *It's Not Me, It's You* was published by Southword Editions in 2019. He blogs at briankirkwriter.com.

JOSEPH LENNON was born in Newport, Rhode Island, and grew up in Rochester, a small town in central Illinois. He has lived in Ireland and Italy and travelled throughout India. After a decade in New York City, teaching at Manhattan College, he now lives in Philadelphia with his family and is Director of Irish Studies at Villanova University. He has published poetry and critical essays on Irish literature and postcolonial studies. His book *Irish Orientalism: A Literary and Intellectual History* (Syracuse UP, 2004) won the Donald J. Murphy Prize for Distinguished First Book from the American Conference for Irish Studies. His poetry collection *Fell Hunger* was published by Salmon in 2011. Lennon spent many years living with undiagnosed coeliac disease and its effects.

RAINA J. LEÓN, PhD is Black, Puerto Rican, and from Philadelphia. She is a member of the Carolina African American Writers Collective, Cave Canem, CantoMundo, Macondo, AfroSurreal Writers Workshop, and Círculo de Poetas and Writers. She is the author of *Canticle of Idols, Boogeyman Dawn, sombra: dis(locate)*, and two chapbooks, *profeta without refuge* and most recently *Areyto to Atabey: Essays on the Mother(ing) Self.* She is a founding editor of *The Acentos Review.*

MICHAEL LONGLEY's twelve collections have received many awards including the Queen's Gold Medal for Poetry and the TS Eliot Prize. His most recent collection *The Candlelight Master* was published in August 2020. He is now completing his thirteenth. In 2015 he was made a Freeman of the City of Belfast.

VICTOR LUFTIG is a Professor teaching in the Department of English at the University of Virginia. Luftig is the author of *Seeing Together, Heterosexual Friendship in English Writing, from Mill to Woolf* (Stanford UP, 1993) and co-editor, with Robert Spoo and Mark Wollaeger, of *Joyce and the Subject of History* (University of Michigan, 1996). He has written many articles and reviews about Irish writing and other topics. He taught at Yale from 1988 to 1994, at Brandeis from 1994 to 1999, and during 19 summers at Middlebury College's Bread Loaf School of English.

PHIL LYNCH's poems have appeared in a range of literary journals and anthologies and have been featured in various radio broadcasts. He performs his work at poetry/spoken word events in Ireland and has performed at events in the USA, UK, Belgium and France. His collection *In a Changing Light* (Salmon Poetry) was published in 2016.

THOMAS LYNCH is the author of four collections of poems, three books of essays and a book of stories, *Apparition & Late Fictions. The Undertaking* won the American Book Award and was a finalist for the National Book Award. His work has appeared in *The Atlantic* and *Granta, The New Yorker* and *Esquire, Poetry* and *The Paris Review*, also *The Times* (of New York, Los Angelus, London and Ireland) and has been the subject of two documentary films, *Learning Gravity* by Cathal Black and PBS Frontline's *The Undertaking*. He lives in Milford, Michigan and Moveen, West Clare. In 2012, Salmon published *The Sin-Eater: A Breviary.*

JOAN McBREEN is from Sligo and for many years has divided her time between Renvyle and Tuam, Co. Galway. She has published five collections of poetry and edited two anthologies, *The White Page/ An Bhileog Bhán* and *The Watchful Heart.* Her most recent collection, *Map and Atlas* was published by Salmon Poetry in 2017. She is currently working on a sixth collection to be published by Salmon.

THOMAS McCARTHY was educated at UCC and worked for many years at Cork City Libraries. His collections include *The First Convention, The Sorrow Garden, Lost Province, Merchant Prince* and *The Last Geraldine Officer*. His *Pandemonium*, 2016, was shortlisted for the Irish Times/Poetry Now Award and his latest collection, *Prophecy*, was published in 2019. He has won the Patrick Kavanagh Award, the Alice Hunt Bartlett Prize and the O'Shaughnessy Prize for Poetry as well as the American-Ireland Funds Annual Literary Award. He has been a member of Aosdána since 1997.

AFRIC McGLINCHEY is the author of *The lucky star of hidden things* and *Ghost of the Fisher Cat* (Salmon Poetry), which were translated into Italian and published by L'Arcolaio. A chapbook, *Invisible Insane* (SurVision) appeared in 2019. She received an Arts Council bursary to research her forthcoming auto-fictional memoir.

MEDBH McGUCKIAN was born in 1950 in Belfast where she continues to live. She has been Writer-in-Residence at Queen's University, Belfast, the University of Ulster, Coleraine, and Trinity College, Dublin, and was Visiting Fellow at the University of California, Berkeley. Her most recent publication, *Marine Cloud Brightening*, was published by Gallery Press in 2019 and shortlisted for the 2020 Irish Times Poetry Now Award.

ETHNA McKIERNAN has been twice awarded a Minnesota State Arts Board grant in poetry. Her first book, *Caravan*, was nominated for the Minnesota Book Award and her work has been widely anthologized. McKiernan has three books published by Salmon Poetry who will also bring out her *Selected Poems* in 2022. McKiernan works in Street Outreach for a non-profit serving the Minneapolis homeless population.

DEVON McNAMARA has published poetry, essays, reviews and interviews in *The Christian Science Monitor, The Hiram Poetry Review, The Laurel Review*, and other publications, created/hosted the West Virginia Public Radio interview/college course, *Women and Literature*, and is on the English faculty at West Virginia Wesleyan College for which she directs May Term Ireland. She teaches in its MFA program for which she also directs the Irish MFA residencies. Her poetry collection, *Driving*, is forthcoming from Salmon Poetry, and a new collection, *Barefoot through Security* is nearing completion.

MARY MADEC received her M.A. in Old English poetry from NUI, Galway and her doctorate in Linguistics from the University of Pennsylvania. She is currently Director of the Villanova Study Abroad Program at NUI, Galway. She won the Hennessy XO Prize for Emerging Poetry in 2008. Her first collection *In Other*

Words, was published by Salmon Poetry in 2010. Her latest, *The Egret Lands With News From Other Parts* was published by Salmon in 2019. She also edited *Jessica Casey & Other Stories* from Salmon Poetry, 2011, showcasing work from people with intellectual disabilities following a multi-award winning project funded by an Arts Participation Bursary from the Arts Council of Ireland. Recently she has worked with immigrant writers. She is also a member of a collective of poets who, through poetry readings, reach to women who have had breast cancer and a co-author of their book *Bosom Pals* published by Doire Press in 2017.

MÁIGHRÉAD MEDBH has published eight poetry books and one of mixed genre. After her first book in 1990, she worked mainly in performance, until Salmon published her historical verse narrative, *Tenant*, in 1999. Her latest book is *Imbolg*, published by Arlen House in November 2020. maighreadmedbh.ie

PAULA MEEHAN's *As If By Magic: Selected Poems* was published in October, 2020. Her books have garnered both popular and critical acclaim in Ireland and internationally. She was Ireland Professor of Poetry from 2013 to 2016—*Imaginary Bonnets with Real Bees in Them*, UCD Press, collects her public lectures from that time.

CHRISTOPHER MERRILL has published six collections of poetry and six books of nonfiction, including, *Only the Nails Remain: Scenes from the Balkan Wars* and *Self-Portrait with Dogwood*. As director of the University of Iowa's International Writing Program, Merrill has conducted cultural diplomacy missions to more than fifty countries.

GERALDINE MITCHELL's fourth collection, *Mute/Unmute*, was published by Arlen House in November 2020. She is a Patrick Kavanagh Award winner and her previous collections are *World Without Maps* (2011), *Of Birds and Bones* (2014) and *Mountains for Breakfast* (2017). Geraldine lives on the Co. Mayo coast.

KELLY MOFFETT is an Associate Professor of English at Northern Kentucky University. Her poems have appeared in journals such as *Rattle, Colorado Review, MidAmerican Review, Cortland Review,* and *Cincinnati Review*. She has one collection through Salmon and one forthcoming and is very proud to be one of Jessie's poets.

NOEL MONAHAN has published eight collections of poetry. His most recent collection *Chalk Dust* was adapted for stage and directed by Padraic McIntyre, Ramor Theatre, 2019. Jessie Lendennie published Monahan's first poem, "The Bishop's Gallop", in *The Salmon* journal, No.15, Summer 1986.

ALAN JUDE MOORE is from Dublin. His most recent collection is *Zinger* (Salmon 2013).

SINÉAD MORRISSEY is the author of six poetry collections. Her selected poems, *Found Architecture*, was published by Carcanet in May 2020.

JOHN MURPHY's third book of poetry is *Zeppelin Vending Machine Manifesto*. His second book was the multi-award winning collection *The Language Hospital* which won the Strokestown International Poetry Prize twice (2015, 2016). His first collection was *The Book Of Water*. All three books are published by Salmon Poetry.

Originally from Armagh, JOAN NEWMANN was a member of the Philip Hobsbaum Belfast Group which included James Simmons and Seamus Heaney and was at the centre of the poetry renaissance in Northern Ireland in the 1960s. Her collections include *Coming of Age* (The Blackstaff Press, 1995); *Thin Ice* (Abbey Press, 1999); *Belongings* (with Kate Newmann) (Arlen House, 2007) and *Prone* (Summer Palace Press, 2007). She is co-founder with her daughter Kate of Summer Palace Press, and was the recipient of the Samhain International Poetry Festival's Craobh na hÉigse Award in 2004.

EILÉAN NÍ CHUILLEANÁIN was born in Cork City in 1942, educated there and at Oxford before spending her working life as an academic in Trinity College, Dublin. She was a founder member of *Cyphers*, a literary journal. She has won the Patrick Kavanagh Award, the Irish Times Award for Poetry, the O'Shaughnessy Award of the Irish-American Cultural Institute which called her "among the very best poets of her generation", and the International Griffin Poetry Prize. Her collections include *Acts and Monuments* (1972, winner of the 1973 Patrick Kavanagh Award), *Site of Ambush* (1975), *The Second Voyage* (1977, 1986), *The Rose Geranium* (1981), *The Magdalene Sermon* (1989) which was shortlisted for the Irish Times/Aer Lingus Award, *The Brazen Serpent* (1994), *The Girl Who Married the Reindeer* (2001), *The Sun-fish* (2009, winner of the 2010 Griffin International Poetry Prize and a Poetry Book Society Recommendation and *The Mother House* (2019) winner of the 2020 Irish Times Poetry Now Award. Her *Collected Poems* were published in October 2020.

KERRIE O'BRIEN is a writer and photographer from Dublin. Her debut collection of poetry *Illuminate* was published by Salmon Poetry in 2016 and made possible by a Literature Bursary from the Arts Council of Ireland. For more visit kerrieobrien.com

CLAIRR O'CONNOR, poet, playwright, novelist, has written five collections of poetry, the latest of which is *Caesura* (Astrolabe 2017). Her third novel *Finding Home* (2020) is now available on Amazon.co.uk. Her radio plays have been broadcast by BBC Radio 4, RTE Radio 1 and Radio Warsaw.

EDWARD O'DWYER is from Limerick and is the author of two poetry collections, *The Rain on Cruise's Street* (2014) and *Bad News, Good News, Bad News* (2017), both from Salmon Poetry. Most recently, he is the author of a short fiction collection, *Cheat Sheets* (2018), published by Truth Serum Press.

JANE O'HANLON is the Education Officer with Poetry Ireland/Éigse Éireann, co-ordinating its education and outreach work. She is a former board member of Children's Books Ireland and of IMRAM bilingual Festival, and a former tutor on the NYCI Certificate in Youth Arts.

NESSA O'MAHONY is from Dublin. She has published five volumes of poetry, including three with Salmon Poetry. Her most recent book is *The Hollow Woman and the Island* (Salmon, 2019).

MARY O'MALLEY has published nine books of poetry, the latest, *Gaudent Angeli* from Carcanet in 2019. She has lectured in NUI Galway for many years and was Trinity College Writer Fellow for 2019. She has won a number of awards, is published in several languages, is working on a book of essays and a prose book, both on the subject of place. She was awarded the Heimbold Chair of Irish Studies at the University of Villanova in 2013 and has held residencies in Paris, Spain and the US. She was writer in resident on the Celtic Explorer, a marine research ship, in 2007 and *Valparaiso* was written in part on the ship. She is a member of Aosdána.

JAMES O'SULLIVAN lectures at University College Cork. His poetry has been published in a variety of journals, including *The Stinging Fly, The SHOp, Cyphers, Banshee,* and *Southword*. His most recent collection of poetry is *Courting Katie* (Salmon, 2017). See jamesosullivan.org for more.

ALICE PETTWAY is the author of *The Time of Hunger, Moth* and *Station Lights* (forthcoming from Salmon Poetry). Her poetry has appeared in *AGNI, The Bitter Oleander, The Colorado Review, Poet Lore, River Styx, The Southern Review, The Threepenny Review* and many others. Currently, Pettway lives and writes near Seattle, Washington.

STEPHEN ROGER POWERS started writing poetry almost twenty years ago to pass time in the middle of the night when he was too energized to sleep after coming off the stage in comedy clubs. He is the author of three poetry collections and a collection of short stories.

LIZ QUIRKE's collection, *The Road Slowly*, was published by Salmon in 2018. She was the winner of the 2017 Listowel Writers' Week Originals Short Poem Competition, the 2016 Dromineer Literary Festival Flash Fiction Competition, the 2015 Poems for Patience competition and the 2012 Doneraile Literary Festival Edmund Spenser Poetry Prize. She was shortlisted for the Cúirt New Writing Prize in 2015 and nominated for a Hennessy Literary Award in 2016. She holds degrees from University College Cork, Dublin City University and NUI Galway. She is a PhD researcher at NUI Galway.

ELIZABETH REAPY is from Mayo and is the author of novels *Red Dirt* and *Skin*. She won Newcomer of the Year at the 2016 Irish Book Awards and in 2017 she was awarded The Rooney Prize for Irish Literature. She is currently working on a feature length screenplay.

Former editor of *Éire-Ireland* and *New Hibernia Review*, THOMAS DILLON REDSHAW writes occasionally for the *Irish Times, The Stinging Fly*, and *Poetry Ireland*. He edited *Well Dreams: Essays on John Montague* (Creighton University Press, 2004).

BERTHA ROGERS lives in New York's Catskill Mountain Region. Her Salmon poetry collections include *Wild, Again* (2019) and *Heart Turned Back* (2010). Her translation of *Beowulf*, the Anglo-Saxon epic, was published in 2000; and her translation with illuminations of the riddle-poems in the Exeter Book, *Uncommon Creatures*, was published in 2019.

CAROL RUMENS lives and writes in North Wales. Her most recent poetry collection is *The Mixed Urn* (Sheep Meadow Press, USA, 2019). *Bezdelki: Small Things* (The Emma Press, UK, 2018) won that year's Michael Marks Award for Best Pamphlet. She contributes a popular blog, *Poem of the Week*, to Guardian Books Online.

LEX RUNCIMAN understands Salmon Poetry's enterprise and vision as unique in contemporary small press publishing. Profoundly Irish in its essence, Salmon's reach is international in scope. *Unlooked For*, Runciman's fourth book with Salmon, is forthcoming. He lives in Portland, Oregon.

MICHAEL SCHMIDT FRSL, poet, scholar, critic and translator, was born in Mexico in 1947; he studied at Harvard and at Wadham College, Oxford, before settling in England. Among his many publications are several collections of poems and a novel, *The Colonist* (1981), about a boy's childhood in Mexico. He is general editor of *PN Review* and founder as well as managing director of Carcanet Press. He lives in Manchester, England.

JOHN W. SEXTON's most recent collection is *Visions at Templeglantine* (Revival Press, 2020). His 2018 collection, *Futures Pass*, was published by Salmon Poetry, who will also publish his next, *The World Under the World*. In 2007 he was awarded a Patrick and Katherine Kavanagh Fellowship in Poetry.

LORNA SHAUGHNESSY has published three poetry collections, *Torching the Brown River, Witness Trees* and *Anchored* (Salmon Poetry), and a chapbook, *Song of the Forgotten Shulamite* (Lapwing). She is also a translator of Spanish and Latin American Poetry and lectures in Hispanic Studies, NUI Galway.

EILEEN SHEEHAN is from County Kerry. Anthology publications include *The Watchful Heart: A New Generation of Irish Poets* (editor Joan McBreen / Salmon Poetry) and *The Deep Heart's Core: Irish Poets Revisit a Touchstone Poem* (editors Eugene O'Connell & Pat Boran / Dedalus Press). Her most recent collection is *The Narrow Way of Souls* (Salmon Poetry)

KNUTE SKINNER, born in St. Louis, Missouri, has had a home in County Clare since 1963. Salmon has published nine of his poetry books as well as a memoir. His latest books from Salmon are *Concerned Attentions* (2013), *The Life That I Have* (2018), and *An Upside Down World* (2019). He has recently celebrated his 91st birthday.

JO SLADE is a poet & painter. Author of six collections of poetry & two chapbooks of poems. *The Painter's House* published by Salmon Poetry 2013 was joint winner of the Michael Hartnett Poetry Prize 2014. Her recent collection *Cycles and Lost Monkeys* was published by Salmon Poetry 2019.

DAMIAN SMYTH's collections are *Downpatrick Races* (2000), *The Down Recorder* (2004), *Lamentations* (2010), *Market Street* (2010), *Mesopotamia* (Templar, 2014) and *English Street* (Templar, 2018). *Irish Street* is due in 2021. He is Head of Literature and Drama with the Arts Council of Northern Ireland in Belfast.

GERARD SMYTH has published ten collections of poetry, the most recent of which are *The Sundays of Eternity* and *A Song of Elsewhere* (both Dedalus Press). *The Yellow River* (with artwork by Seán McSweeney) was published by Solstice Arts Centre, Navan. He is a member of Aosdána.

A. E. STRINGER is the author of four collections of poems, most recently *Asbestos Brocade* (Salmon Poetry, 2017). His work has appeared in such journals as *The Nation, Antaeus,* and *The Ohio Review.* For twenty-four years, he taught writing and literature at Marshall University. He lives, writes, and makes music in Huntington, West Virginia.

ANNE TANNAM is the author of two poetry collections, with a third *Twenty-six Letters of a New Alphabet* forthcoming with Salmon. For more information or to contact Anne, visit her website annetannampoetry.ie

CAROLYN L. TIPTON teaches at U.C. Berkeley. She has won fellowships from both the N.E.H. and the N.E.A. Her first book, *To Painting: Poems by Rafael*

Alberti, won the National Translation Award. Her second book of translated poems by Alberti, *Returnings: Poems of Love and Distance*, won the Cliff Becker Translation Prize. Her third book, *The Poet of Poet Laval*, a collection of original poetry, has recently been published by Salmon Poetry.

DANIEL TOBIN is the author of nine books of poems, including *The Stone in the Air* (Salmon), his versions from the German of Paul Celan and *Blood Labors*, named a Best Poetry Book of the year by the *New York Times* in 2018. His poetry has won many awards, among them the Julia Ward Howe Prize, the Meringoff Award, the Massachusetts Book Award, and fellowships from the NEA and Guggenheim Foundation. His most recent book of essays is *On Serious Earth*.

PETER VAN DE KAMP was born in The Hague in 1956. He came to Ireland in 1981. He has published 18 books, and is finishing his 19th (*Whodunnit in Dubliners*). Salmon published two of his collections of verse, *Notes* (1999) and *In Train* (2008). Peter teaches at the Munster University of Technology.

DRUCILLA WALL was raised in Philadelphia, Pennsylvania. She received her B.A. from the University of Wisconsin, her M.A. from the University of Nebraska-Omaha, and her Ph.D. in English from the University of Nebraska at Lincoln. She teaches poetry and essay writing, and Native American literature, at the University of Missouri-St. Louis. In addition to poetry, her essays appear in journals and anthologies. She has earned awards and fellowships for her work, including the Mari Sandoz Prairie Schooner Short Story Award, the Western Literature Association Willa Pilla Prize for Humor in Writing, and University of Nebraska Fling and Larson Fellowships. She lives in St. Louis, Missouri, and has spent summers with family and friends in Wexford and Galway, Ireland, since 1985. Her debut collection, *The Goose at the Gates*, was published by Salmon in 2011.

EAMONN WALL is a native of Co. Wexford who has lived in the USA since 1982. In addition to his six volumes of poetry published by Salmon, Eamonn Wall has written two prose books: *Writing the Irish West: Ecologies and Traditions* (2011) and *From the Sin-é Café to the Black Hills: Notes on the New Irish* (2000). His most recent poetry collection, *Junction City: New & Selected Poems 1990-2015* was published by Salmon in 2015. He lives in Missouri where he is employed by the University of Missouri-St. Louis as a professor of International Studies and English. Eamonn Wall serves on the board of Irish American Writers and Artists Inc., an organization founded to foster and promote the work of Irish American writers and artists. He is also a founder of Scallta Media—an initiative to promote the work of up-and-coming Co. Wexford creative artists. *Eamonn Wall: Your Rivers Have Trained You*, a documentary on his career as a writer directed by Paul O'Reilly, was released last year by Lowland Films.

GORDON WALMSLEY is the author of seven books of poetry, the last four of which have been published by Salmon. His *Selected Poems* (Octave) is due to appear in the Spring. He is also the author of the poetically constructed tale *Daisy, The Alchemical Adventures of a New Orleans Hermaphrodite*. His poems have been translated into various languages, more recently in Italian (*Poesie Scelte, Selected Poems*) in a bilingual edition published in Catania.

SANDRA ANN WINTERS is the winner of the 2011 Gregory O'Donoghue International Poetry Competition, and a Pushcart nominee twice. She is the author of two full-length poetry collections by Salmon Poetry: *The Place Where I Left You* (2014), and *Do Not Touch* (2020).

JOSEPH WOODS' most recent poetry collection is *Monsoon Diary*. He is Poetry Ireland's longest-serving director, during which time he worked closely with Jessie Lendennie and Salmon Poetry and holds both in high regard and friendship. He now lives with his family in Harare, Zimbabwe.

SANDRA YANNONE's poems and reviews have found sanctuary in *Ploughshares, Poetry Ireland Review, Impossible Archetype, Lambda Literary Review*, and elsewhere. Salmon Poetry published her debut collection *Boats for Women* in 2019 and will publish *The Glass Studio* in 2022. She hosts Cultivating Voices LIVE Poetry on Facebook. Visit sandrayannone.com.

JESSIE LENDENNIE was born in Blytheville, Arkansas. She is co-founder (1981) and Managing Director of Salmon Poetry, for which she has commissioned and published over 600 volumes of poetry as well as a select list of literary criticism, drama, fiction, memoir and essays. Her own publications include a book-length prose poem *Daughter* (1988), reprinted as *Daughter and Other Poems* in 2001 and a collection of poetry, *Walking Here* (2011). She compiled and edited: *The Salmon Guide to Creative Writing in Ireland* (1990); *Salmon: A Journey in Poetry, 1981-2007* (2007); *Poetry: Reading it, Writing It, Publishing It* (2009); *Dogs Singing: A Tribute Anthology* (2010); and *Even The Daybreak: 35 Years of Salmon Poetry* (2016). Her poetry has also been anthologised in *Irish Poetry Now: Other Voices, Unveiling Treasures, The Attic Guide To The Published Works of Irish Women Literary Writers* and *The White Page/An Bhileog Bhán: Twentieth-Century Irish Women Poets*, among others. Her poems, essays and articles have been widely published and she has given numerous readings, lectures and writing courses in Ireland and abroad, including Yale University; Rutgers University; The Irish Embassy, Washington D.C; The University of Alaska, Fairbanks and Anchorage; MIT, Boston; The Loft, Minneapolis, MN; Café Teatre, Copenhagen, Denmark; the University of Arkansas, Fayetteville; The Irish American Cultural Centre, Chicago and The Bowery Poetry Club, New York City. She regularly attends the AWP Association of Writers and Writing Programs Conference in the US, where Salmon is a prominent presence, having been shortlisted for the Small Press Publisher of the Year AWP in 2015. In 2012, she opened *The Salmon Bookshop & Literary Centre* in Ennistymon, Co. Clare, a vibrant hub for literary events, for writers, readers, students & academics, and the base from which Salmon Poetry runs its publishing operation. www.thesalmonbookshop.com

Jessie Lendennie with her mother Willie Mae Harbin Lendennie,
San Francisco, 1956

BOOKS BY JESSIE LENDENNIE

Poetry Collections

Daughter (1988)   *Daughter & Other Poems* (2001)   *Walking Here* (2011)

As Editor

  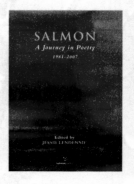

The Salmon Guide to Poetry   *The Salmon Guide to Creative*   *Salmon: A Journey in Poetry*
Publishing in Ireland (1989)   *Writing in Ireland* (1991)   *1981–2007* (2007)

Poetry: Reading it, Writing   *Dogs Singing: A Tribute*   *Even The Daybreak:*
It, Publishing It (2009)   *Anthology* (2010)   *35 Years of Salmon Poetry*
                                                              (2016)

salmonpoetry40

Publishing Irish & International Poetry Since 1981

The Salmon Bookshop
& Literary Centre
Ennistymon, County Clare, Ireland

"Another wonderful Clare outlet."
The Irish Times, 35 Best Independent Bookshops